So Much More

Love and Light,

So Much More

A Poignant Memoir about Finding Love, Fighting Adversity, and Defining Life on My Own Terms

ZULEMA ARROYO FARLEY

ATRIA BOOKS

New York London Toronto Sydney New Delhi

ATRIA
BOOKS

An Imprint of Simon & Schuster, Inc.
1230 Avenue of the Americas
New York, NY 10020

First Atria Books hardcover edition September 2019

ATRIA BOOKS and colophon are trademarks
of Simon & Schuster, Inc.

For information about special discounts for bulk purchases,
please contact Simon & Schuster Special Sales at 1-866-506-1949
or business@simonandschuster.com.

The Simon & Schuster Speakers Bureau can bring authors
to your live event. For more information, or to book an event,
contact the Simon & Schuster Speakers Bureau at 1-866-248-3049
or visit our website at www.simonspeakers.com.

Manufactured in the United States of America

1   3   5   7   9   10   8   6   4   2

Library of Congress Cataloging-in-Publication
data has been applied for.

ISBN 978-1-5011-8805-3
ISBN 978-1-5011-8807-7 (ebook)

TO THE FOUR LOVES OF MY LIFE:
*To Nick, my Mr. Bond, for keeping
the promise, in sickness and in health.
To Jameel and Andrea, who have taught me
unconditional love to unimaginable lengths.
To Dad, for guiding me from the Spirit world.*

Contents

Introduction

Ever since I was a little girl growing up in Mayagüez, Puerto Rico, I have dreamed of becoming a writer.

When I was six years old, one of the three presents I asked for from the *Reyes Magos*—the Three Wise Men who visited Jesus after he was born, bearing gifts of gold, frankincense, and myrrh—was a typewriter. That red Sears children's typewriter was the first of four typewriters I ended up owning.

I kept journals. Wrote long letters to faraway pen pals. I loved writing essays for English lessons. Nothing felt better than sitting down in front of a blank piece of paper and letting my thoughts guide the pen.

I told my high school English teacher, Mrs. Mora, that I planned to be an author one day. But, beyond words, I was also obsessed with writing paraphernalia, pens and ink, not ⌐⌐⌐⌐⌐ds of stationery. I think I kept the stationery ⌐⌐⌐⌐ez Mall in business for a few years! I en-⌐⌐⌐⌐teen, skipping first-year English courses ⌐⌐⌐⌐ because of all the time I spent writing

⌐⌐⌐⌐write a book about my life. But first ⌐⌐⌐⌐ live it. No matter what the angle, I always thought my book's focus would be about my unicorn life—a big life, the sexy and cinematic stuff that made me grateful to be alive and in my skin.

While in college, my organizational management professor asked the class to think about what defined each one of us and to write a five-thousand-word autobiography. This prompted me to sketch out a twenty-page book proposal—a book describing my life up until then. I never submitted that proposal or got to write the book back in college. I knew that it was not the right time. There was *so much more* to experience before I put pen to paper.

Twenty years later I finally did submit my book proposal, but by then my life story was vastly different from the one I had considered writing while in college.

Nothing is more unpredictable than life itself.

Not even two years after tying the knot with the love of my life, Nick, in the most awesome idyllic wedding ever, embarking on what I wholeheartedly believed would be our happily ever after, I received life-changing news: I had cancer. Not a known cancer—that would be boring—but a rare, poorly researched, and potentially life-threatening cancer called sarcoma. Sarcoma is considered an "orphan" cancer, as fewer than 200,000 people in the United States are diagnosed with it. In short, I had won the Powerball jackpot of all cancers, a ticket I surely did not want to have! As you can imagine, my world turned upside down.

My time with my one and only, Nick, became a ticking clock of moments and memories that we wanted to experience together before we no longer could. Our ride in this world rushed to the forefront of our priorities; nothing and no one else mattered. It was no longer about planning the future but about *living* it. Together, Nick and I discovered a new normal as we tried to make as much of the time we had left together extraordinary. I felt charged to start spending my remaining hours on *my* terms—and I would allow no disease, doctor, friend, family member, or well-meaning stranger to dictate what that meant.

I have traveled, I have read, I have partied, I have danced; I have loved and been loved. For nearly two years I have written this book about how Nick and I created a "life list" of sparkling, effervescent moments we insisted on spending together, come hell or high water. And along the way I have discovered something infinite, something brighter, than what I thought possible in life. My spiritual playing field expanded. There has always been something different about me I couldn't put my finger on, a divine guidance intervening all the time in my thoughts and life. *This* would be my story to tell.

I want to say, too, that I feel my story is important not because it is *my* story but because it is the story of how we must all find joy in the face of conflict and challenge. Life happens to every one of us, and when it is painful, you have a choice either to give in to the brokenness you feel or to stare it down with love and good intentions. For me, cancer was my ultimate challenge, but for you it may be living with chronic disease, losing the job you have had all your life, experiencing anxiety, losing a close friend or family member, deciding to get divorced, or getting your heart broken into a million little pieces.

My deepest desire is for this memoir to inspire and uplift anyone who is struggling with their own challenges, especially a health-related one, or is close to someone who is. If you have a list of passions or goals, even just a few, that you need to accomplish before the end of the year, before you turn fifty, before you get married or have kids, or even before you die, don't wait until a scary diagnosis arrives to start making it happen. Take charge. Do what you must to fill your mind and heart with happiness. You are the protagonist of your story. Celebrate what it means to embrace life to the fullest and with those you love. Don't let setbacks turn you into a victim. I have never felt sorry for myself, and that's been one of my saving graces (second only to champagne—lots and lots of champagne). Let go of your fears, dare to dream, and embrace your passions, whatever they may be. When you stop worrying about what could happen and what other people think and focus on creating your future, opportunities that you hadn't anticipated will often present themselves. And sometimes, those opportunities can steer you in a direction you could never have foreseen . . . But I'll share a lot more on that later.

The truth is that I live every day knowing that my life has a looming expiration date. Some doctors believe it's not a matter of *if* my cancer will return but *when*. So, in the now, in

1

A Little Black Dress

One is never overdressed or underdressed
with a Little Black Dress.

—KARL LAGERFELD

A few days shy of my thirty-seventh birthday, January 16, 2010, I spent the afternoon with my maternal grandmother, Abuela Esperanza, up in the Bronx, reminiscing, playing *lotería*, and eating Puerto Rican staple dishes like *arroz con habichuelas* and *carne guisada*. Even though I was having a great time, my mind kept wandering to the romantic date I had planned for later that night with a man named Nick. We'd gone out on our first date three days earlier and he had already swept me off my stilettos. By the time I said goodbye to my *abuela,* the monarch butterflies in my stomach were taking flight.

I took my time getting ready because I knew things with Nick were going to be special. Something felt different with him. Even though we'd seen each other twice in three days, I couldn't wait to see him again. Before leaving for the date, I stopped to look at myself in the mirror. My Oscar de la Renta dress fit as if it were bespoke, hugging my Latina curves in all the right places. Satisfied, I stepped out into the Manhattan night.

When the elevator door slid open to Nick's penthouse, I took only one step forward to find him waiting for me with a huge smile. He greeted me with a gentle kiss, took off my coat, grabbed my hand, and led me into the lounge area. Then he disappeared.

I settled into Nick's dark gray modern sofa and readjusted my long, dark brown hair over my shoulders. When he reappeared, he was carrying a large Bergdorf Goodman box with a giant purple bow. He placed it on my lap. I stared up at him in disbelief, then looked down at the gift. I carefully removed the lid, slowly ruffling through the tissue paper as the beat of my heart drummed along to a Gotan Project song playing on his Naim sound system. He looked on with a sweet grin as I unfolded a finely detailed sleeveless black dress. It had an elegant plunge neck with romantic silk floral lace adornments, a sexy accentuated waist, and a full, poufy miniskirt, to show off what I think is one of my best physical assets: my legs. It was very Carrie Bradshaw from *Sex and the City* and perfectly captured my spirit. But my biggest surprise came when I noticed the designer. *Ah, look at that.* Nick had remembered. In wear it for my birthday celebration later in the week—but I loved it so much that I didn't want to wait another second to put it on! Knowing that we had dinner reservations in fifteen minutes, I grabbed my Chanel clutch and the dress and rushed to the bathroom to change outfits.

Closing the door behind me, I placed the handbag on the vanity, then stared in disbelief at the gown in my hands with worry: *What if it doesn't fit?* I hastily undressed, slipped it on, then breathed a sigh of relief. The dress fit perfectly. I felt like a modern-day Cinderella, who I am pretty sure would have taken a stunning high fashion designer dress over a silly glass shoe if given the chance! How did Nick know it would fit? He must have taken a peek at my dress size on one of our previous nights together. Nick was clearly a great listener with a keen eye, just another one of the qualities I already loved about him.

That last thought blew me away. I already *loved* everything about him. *Love? Could this be it?* My mind was racing as I retouched my makeup and rearranged my hair. I took another deep breath, smoothed out the dress, and slipped back into my signature Louboutin sky-high spike stilettos. I took one last glance in the mirror: I wanted to look elegant yet sexy for the man waiting to take me out . . . the man I had gone on a first date with three days ago but had started regularly corresponding with four months earlier . . . the man that I already knew was the One For Me.

I had been "around the block" when it came to love—with heartbreaks, sexy lovers, long-term and short-term beaus, men who shared and furthered my appreciation of the arts, fashion, wine, business, and culture . . . But this? Nick was different. He stirred up depths of emotion that were completely new to me. I felt at ease with him and swore we had met in a past life. I was also wildly, physically attracted to him. I'll be honest: a year earlier I might have said he was not my type! Yet even though Nick's kind, blue eyes, short blondish-brown-gray hair, and average height stood in stark contrast to my usual preferred Mediterranean stereotype—tall, dark, and handsome—it clearly did not matter. Years of dating had finally taught me to throw away the Perfect Man blueprint. Nick was not just a ravishing British gentleman but also a brilliant geek. He had more than thirty years as a Wall Street senior executive under his belt. He was also a seven-time marathon runner, a Formula Honda racer, an avid golfer, an audiophile, and twelve years my senior. Who cared that he could have used a tan? What Nick stirred within me went far beyond any expectation.

Nick and I put on our coats to make our way out to Tribeca's cobblestone streets hand in hand. This was unlike any other third date I had ever been on. Dare I say it was the spooky polar opposite of any other date I had *ever* been on? We initially met in person at the Sean Kelly Gallery in Chelsea during a Gavin Turk exhibition and had stayed in touch since the basics about each other, our knew Nick was divorced with two teenage boys, that he had recently ended an eighteenth-month relationship, and that his senior role at one of the top global investment banks required him to fly all over the world and to London once a month.

Most importantly, we were already friends, and with so many details out of the way, what remained were tantalizing conversations about goals and dreams. We also had explosive physical chemistry. It was a new and electrifying territory that I thought about every day.

After a quick walk on an invigoratingly cold winter night, we reached Nick's favorite neighborhood steak house. The maître d' at Dylan Prime escorted us to our table with a glass of Krug Grande Cuvée champagne, and we settled in for an evening that, unbeknownst to us, would be the first of a lifetime to come. Nick took the lead in ordering, as he had done at our previous two dates that week. He chose his favorite meal: filet mignon with peppercorn sauce, french fries accompanied by wilted spinach, and, to drink, a 1990 Cos d'Estournel. Watching Nick order was a treat; I felt like I had finally found my equal. He knew what he wanted, he was über-confident, and he was chivalrous yet not afraid to take charge. We sh so many qualities, including an unequivocal zest for l a mutual openness and ease came naturally. Our co also flowed seamlessly, with Nick's dry sense of ing me to tears with laughter. His playful, eas a perfect match for my hot-blooded spirit.

As the wine played with our senses, tertained our palates, and our conversa turn into an area we were both wildly e travel. We shared our favorite cities—Paris fo York for Nick—and places we couldn't wait to g like Hong Kong for Nick and the Amalfi Coast for me. We also talked about places where we had never been but yearned to explore, like Bora Bora, Istanbul, and Jordan. There was so much more we wanted to do that it suddenly dawned on us: Why not create our very own "life list" for two—you know, like a bucket list but less maudlin? It made perfect sense at the time, as if we knew that this night and this dinner would be the start of the rest of our lives. A future that included the two of us together suddenly felt like a given.

I opened my iPhone notes app to begin crafting our list. We both thrived on dreaming *big*. It wasn't at all presumptuous to compile an adventurous, colorful, and an admittedly decadent list of goals. What to include? For starters, Nick grew up playing the piano and as a teenager played the oboe in an orchestra and performed Chopin preludes and Beethoven sonatas. I had always wanted to finish the piano lessons I never completed as a child. Typical us, always aiming for the crème de la crème and unwilling to settle; it was only natural that we added "Owning a Steinway concert grand piano" to our list. Privy to my wild obsession for champagne, Nick already knew that "Exploring the Champagne region" was a must; he had visited Champagne many times. When he told me about his fear of heights, I suggested we conquer his fear by skydiving together . . . Anyone else might have recoiled at the idea, but if there's one thing I love about Nick, it is that no challenge is too big, so he readily accepted, and we wrote it down. He then countered with "Skiing in the Alps" and "Scuba diving with my sons." I was quickly on board. He was already a Professional Association of Diving Instructors–certified scuba diver, having dived in the Maldives and the Red Sea, yet I had never even worn a diving mask.

What was most riveting about creating this life list together is that, not only did Nick and I share and write down what we wanted to do, but we also challenged each other to step out of our respective comfort zones and dare to experience the new and unexpected. Even if it was just on paper at the moment, we pushed each other—and each other's imaginations—past our fears and apprehensions to exhilarating new heights, never taking no for an answer, and always aspiring to bigger and better feats. This kind of rapport was exciting, sexy, and challenging for me. This list showed me that if I were to have any kind of future with Nick, our lives would hardly be dull.

As the waiter removed our dinner plates, we savored the last drops of claret, and I came face-to-face with a realization that hit me like a breath of fresh air: I had found my kindred spirit. A thrilling life of shared passions and achievements was coming into focus, clear as day. Nick effused a kind of certainty and confidence that I found very intriguing—he reminded me of James Bond—and brought out a daring side in me too. As if someone had whispered into my ear, I heard an inner voice tell me that nothing could get in our way as long as we remained together. I had a solid sense that Nick was the man I wanted to venture out into the world with; the man I wanted to be part of my joys and fears; the man I wanted to spend the rest of my life with, holding hands until we grew old.

As the evening came to a close, we wandered back to Nick's Tribeca penthouse. There was no sense of urgency, only gentle, relaxed, and contented peace. We figured our blossoming relationship, much like the list we had just come up with, was something we'd move through slowly and steadily—the latter being a tangible, casual reminder and catalog of all the fun to be had together.

We had just created a list that would soon become our life's road map, urging us to suck the marrow out of life even when my days on earth felt numbered.

2

Death Awakens

The life of the dead is placed
in the memory of the living.
—MARCUS TULLIUS CICERO

When I was born, I almost died.

It was January 19, 1973, in Mayagüez. Mayagüez is located on the lush western side of Puerto Rico. It's the fourth-largest city on the island, and in 1973 the population was about 85,000. The city is most famous for the Nuestra Señora de la Candelaria cathedral. The impressive Plaza de Colón statue, a tribute to Christopher Columbus, who is said to have discovered Puerto Rico on his second voyage to the Americas, landing at Mayagüez, stands in the middle of the square. The city is surrounded by mountains on one side and Mar Caribe on the other.

Except for the usual nausea in her first three months, my Mami, Paola, had enjoyed a smooth pregnancy. She was a stunningly gorgeous nineteen-year-old—a vibrant woman with fair skin and long beautiful waves of blond-brown hair. Her slender figure and fine features certainly turned heads in the town! She was happily married to my Papi, Edwin Arroyo Mora, six years her senior. Papi was dark skinned with Indio

Taino features and dark brown curly hair that he kept closely trimmed. He had a wide smile and you could not fail to notice how his bright white teeth flashed when he laughed.

My parents had met five years earlier at a typical *fiesta de marquesina* (our term for a house party; *marquesina* means porch or awning) to celebrate the birthday of a mutual friend. Papi spotted my mother right away. She was fifteen and he was twenty-one. Their love flourished, mostly through chaperoned dates, which were customary at the time in traditional Catholic families. These were mainly formal visits in my mother's living room with her family. However, Mami confessed later, she occasionally snuck out to watch Papi as he drove his blue 1956 Chevy in clandestine street races along the back roads of town. Exciting! Papi's mother, Candelaria, was a tall, fair-skinned woman with curly dark hair, heavy European-like features, and a personality and demeanor that earned her a reputation for being tough, strict, and sometimes unfriendly. For reasons which were never revealed, Candelaria did not approve of the relationship. One day, much to her dismay, Papi announced his intention to marry Mami. For people who knew Candelaria, they were not entirely surprised that she would object even though Mami and Papi clearly loved each other deeply. My father eventually persuaded his mother to accompany him to my mother's home to ask for Mami's hand in marriage—a testament to Papi's personality and tenacity. The man knew what he wanted, and he went after it—just like me!

Santiago was my maternal grandfather (my *abuelo*), and even though he was a strict and stoic figure who bossed everyone around from his wheelchair, he gave my parents his blessing to be married. Looking back, I think Santiago knew to not "mess" with my Mami. Mami was a tough cookie like him, even at her young age! Santiago found my father to be a charming, well-mannered, poised, and driven young man, as well as a hard worker who could provide for his daughter and future grandchildren. An engagement of just over a year followed to allow Mami to turn eighteen. My mother used the time to plan the wedding, and on October 24, 1971, Mami and Papi were married. My mother always knew exactly what she wanted on her wedding day, and at sixteen years old got herself a job at Tienda El Ensueño, the town's wedding shop. Now, at that time you were not allowed to work until you turned eighteen, but, using her poise and a little coy demeanor, Mami persuaded the shop owners to think she was older than she was. Young in age but wise in years, Mami's practical sense was better than any school education could buy.

Working at Tienda El Ensueño gave my mom the opportunity to buy all the wedding items she needed, from her dress fabric to décor for the reception, allowing my mother to have the wedding of her dreams. Despite her misgivings, Candelaria played seamstress, designing and creating Mami's wedding gown—a modest all-white dress representing purity in the eyes of God based on our family's ardent Catholic beliefs. The lovely dress was accented by a timeless floor-length mantilla, or veil, with French Chantilly lace details.

My parents' traditional ceremony was held at San Benito, a Catholic church, and was followed by a formal breakfast wedding reception, which is very common in European cultures like England and was customary in Puerto Rico at that time. Mami wore bright red lipstick—which made a standout statement—patent white shoes, and a stunning pearl headpiece that framed her beautiful face.

My parents' life together at first began under Candelaria's

roof until they saved up for their own house. After getting married, Mami switched jobs, going to work at Mademoiselle, the town's "it" women's fashion shop, and Papi got a job as the foreman at a construction company. They had planned to have kids as soon as they settled into their own home. By the time Mami became pregnant with me, at eighteen, my parents were more than ready to welcome their first baby.

My parents' life progressed at a gentle pace, the way any expecting couple's might: thinking of names, preparing their home for the baby's arrival, working overtime to save money, spending time with family and friends, and sneaking off on weekend getaways before their world was turned upside down.

What Mami and Papi didn't know was that life was gearing up to throw them a curveball. In the early hours of Friday, January 19, 1973, my mother went into labor. Both she and my father thought they knew what to expect, but nothing could have prepared them for what unfolded that day and what would come in the weeks and months ahead. They rushed to the hospital like any other nervous first-time parents. Their families gathered in the waiting room with bottles of Don Q rum and cigars at the ready to celebrate. Once Mami was admitted and hooked up to monitors in the delivery room, the waiting game began, since she was not dilating very quickly. The ob-gyn said if there were no change in the next few hours, they would likely have to do an unplanned C-section. Hanging on with every breath, timing every contraction, Mami waited as patiently as she could until at long last her body was ready. She finally pushed me out at 1:20 p.m. and I was placed in my mother's arms for the very first time.

Without a worry in the world, Mami tenderly kissed my forehead as only a new mother could and the waiting room burst with excitement. There was applause, then embraces and tears of joy as my parents admired my rosy complexion. My mom tells me that she remembers feeling a wild mix of awe and excitement that likely overwhelms all parents the first time they lay eyes on their first child.

A few hours into this, however, a nurse noticed that my skin had turned from pink to yellow. The team of doctors took me from my Mami's arms and, after quickly examining me, explained I had jaundice, a fairly common occurrence in newborns that signifies low levels of bilirubin. Although jaundice isn't generally considered a life-threatening disease, the doctors admitted me to be safe. When my mother was released from the hospital on Saturday, she left empty-handed. This hospitalization was the first of many that life would have in store for me.

I remained hospitalized for two more days before my bilirubin level stabilized and then my parents took me home to begin our life together as a family. Soon after settling into our daily routine, Mami noticed that every feeding was immediately followed by a violent bout of projectile vomiting. It seemed that I could not hold down food. Distressed at the thought that I wasn't getting the nutrition I needed to survive, my parents took me to see my pediatrician, who was unable to pinpoint what was going on. Mami has never been one to take a question mark for an answer, not even at the age of nineteen. She decided seek a second opinion. Unlike the first doctor, the second pediatrician took a set of X-rays. As he reviewed the images, he turned to Mami, and said, "You have to take your daughter to the hospital immediately." Mami gasped for air.

I often think about what my mother felt at this point in her life. A very young first-time mom going through all the worries and excitement that comes with early motherhood, now overcome with despair and anxiety. Yet she pushed for answers and, no matter what she was feeling, always made my well-being her priority. I believe that I inherited Mami's strength, intuition, and determination. She pressed the doctors for complete answers to her questions so she could make the best decisions about my care. If it were not for her determination and inner strength in the face of adversity, I might not have lived past those first few weeks.

After numerous tests and examinations at the hospital, our doctor discovered that I had been born with a rare condition called pyloric stenosis. The pyloric sphincter functions like a valve and allows food to travel from the stomach to the small intestine, where most nutrient absorption takes place. However, in my case, I was born with my pyloric sphincter closed, so food couldn't reach the next stage of the digestive process, which prevented me from absorbing crucial nutrients. As a result, I was severely dehydrated and needed immediate hospitalization. Surgery came next.

Papi was Mami's rock, yet both were distraught as they helplessly looked at their month-old baby on a gurney, hooked up to an IV. In 1973, operating on a newborn in a Puerto Rican hospital wasn't exactly a calming thought; can you imagine the risk factors? Yet it was the only way doctors could widen my pyloric sphincter to resolve my digestive condition. Yet before they could proceed, they had another hurdle to overcome: the veins in my tiny arms had been poked so many times during the preliminary tests that they could no longer withstand more IV needles. It was imperative that the doctors had access to unobstructed veins to perform the surgery. In these circumstances, the next best spot was to find them in my scalp. They shaved my straight dark brown hair, which

I even had as a baby, and poked around my head, with no luck. So they settled on the most drastic option remaining: a venous cutdown, in which the surgeon surgically exposes the saphenous vein in the leg and inserts a small tube that is then connected to the IV line. It was the first surgery of my life. It was also a surgery that is no longer done today, thanks to the development of safer techniques. I still have the three-inch scar on my leg to show for it—the first of many to come.

My family on both sides are traditionally Catholic, so their immediate coping mechanism was to pray the rosary as the surgeon warned Mami and Papi that a pyloric procedure was considered life-threatening, especially when performed on a four-week-old baby. Fearing I might not survive the surgery, Candelaria rushed out to call the family priest and asked him to baptize me right away: if the operation took a turn for the worst, my family didn't want to leave my soul in limbo! While they waited for the priest to arrive, my parents realized they needed to immediately name my godparents to meet the Catholic church's requirements. They decided on two relatives who had served as the best man and matron of honor at their wedding, my father's uncle Juan and his wife, Zara. As I was rolled into the operating room, Candelaria reappeared with a priest, everyone huddled around my gurney, and I was baptized in the surgery room minutes before going under.

Hours stretched into what felt like an eternity to *mi familia*. But at long last the surgeon emerged from the OR and announced I would be fine. My family breathed a collective sigh of relief and shed tears of joy, although my plight was far from over. Forty-eight hours after my operation, near the hour of my discharge, I ran a high fever. The doctors ran lab work that showed I'd caught an infection in the operating room. It took another week of hospitalization and heavy antibiotics before I could go home.

By the time my two-month birthday came along, I had spent more time in the hospital fighting uncommon health conditions than in my own crib. I had endured two surgeries, a postsurgical infection, and a brush with death. Yet I had survived. As I have *always* survived. Because, even as a fragile baby, my soul's desire to live was far too great. I sometimes think those first two months of struggling to stay alive are what established my strong love of life and filled me with grit and determination.

Back from the hospital, Mami returned to her job at Mademoiselle while Papi continued working as a foreman for a construction company. Not long after, Mami became pregnant with my younger sister, Jessica, my only sibling. Family life continued apace, but it was simply the calm before another major storm.

Saturday, May 11, 1974, began like any other. It was the day before Mother's Day. Already eight months pregnant with Jessica, Mami left me with our next-door neighbor, Doña Emelinda. I called her "Tata." Tata was in her late fifties, and the most loving human on the planet as far as I was concerned. Mami went off to work as usual, hoping to rack up a few more hours before going on maternity leave. Saturdays were normally Papi's day off, but he, too, was looking to pick up extra work to provide some extra cushion for the new baby. A weekend shift was needed to finish up an urgent job, and Papi grabbed the opportunity. Just minutes shy of noon, as his fellow workers and friends were getting ready to wrap up for lunch, he jumped into one of the tractors to get one more task done before joining them so he could hopefully go home early.

Papi steered the tractor up a small ramp. It was a move he had surely done a thousand times before; however, that day he somehow lost control of the machine, and it toppled over the side of a hill and dropped to the ground below. Some of Papi's friends noticed that he had not made it to lunch and went to look for him. They found him crushed under the huge machine. Several of Papi's work buddies desperately tried to lift the enormous tractor off him with their bare hands—an impossible feat. But it was futile: Papi had been killed instantly.

The men followed company protocol by informing the company chief of what happened, and an ambulance, firefighters, and police were called to the scene. Since everyone knew Mami was almost full term, they wanted to avoid putting her and Jessica at risk, so they decided to contact my godfather, Juan, who was listed as an emergency contact. My godparents, God bless them, took it from there. Despite being personally shattered by the news, their priorities were breaking the news to my mom in a way that did not cause her to go into early labor and making sure I was protected from the information and cared for during the aftermath. My godmother, Zara, and Mami shared the same ob-gyn, so Zara's first call was to him. He recommended breaking the news in parts. Coincidentally, Mami had called the ob-gyn office earlier that morning complaining about a pain in her hip, and he had called in a pain reliever to the pharmacy next door to her workplace. Now, given the news of my father's death, he told Zara that he would call the pharmacy to explain the situation and, instead of a pain reliever, to switch the prescription to a tranquilizer.

My godparents made a beeline to my mother's store, and the pharmacist, who had just received the news and instructions from the ob-gyn, called my mom to notify her that the prescription was ready for pickup. Eager to relieve the pain in her hip, my mom told her boss that she was taking a short break to stop by the pharmacy. The intravenous tranquilizer took a little longer than expected, since she had to wait for the pharmacist to administer it. Mami made herself comfortable, happy to finally sit down and rest her sore hip while she could.

Meanwhile, Juan and Zara arrived at her store, briefed Mami's boss on the tragedy, and collected her belongings. It took only twenty steps to get from the shop to the pharmacy, but to Juan it felt like miles away. He was sweating profusely and using his white *pañuelo*, or handkerchief, to repeatedly wipe down his face. He stopped in front of the pharmacy, made the sign of the cross, took a few deep breaths, and slowly pushed open the door. Once inside, Juan and Zara held hands and prayed to God for strength.

Mami, who was casually reading the latest *Vanidades* women's fashion magazine, immediately knew something was wrong when she saw the look on their faces. She turned pale and her heart sank. Although they did their best to soften the blow, telling her that Papi had suffered an accident at work, she still knew it was bad. "*Cuco está muy malito*" ("Cuco is in bad shape"), Juan said, referring to my father by his nickname. "Come with us." Thanks to the tranquilizer, Mami calmly rose from her seat and walked out of the store on Juan's arm. They drove straight to their home, avoiding the obvious topic, until they arrived. Visibly distraught and in tears, Mami sat in Juan and Zara's living room and waited for the news she feared was coming.

"Cuco had a very bad accident at work today at around twelve thirty p.m.," Juan said. "He passed away." Although he tried to stay composed, he felt the room spinning before him and his voice cracking as he uttered the words he could not believe he was saying.

"Can we go see him?" Mami asked almost immediately.

My godfather, Juan, explained that since the accident took place at work and no one knew how it happened, it remained an open police investigation. Papi's body was being processed accordingly, so it was unavailable to the family.

That's when Mami lost it. This couldn't be happening, she thought. Juan and Zara embraced Mami to comfort her as she processed the devastating news. Zara asked Mami whom she wanted to call from her side of the family. Mami gave her the numbers to dial. The list included her older brother, Rafael, who lived in Manhattan at the time. He got on the next flight to San Juan to be by Mami's side. Juan and Zara offered to take care of funeral arrangements, but Mami insisted she would handle them herself. I am not surprised she wanted to honor her beloved's passing on her terms. It was what Papi would have wanted.

When it comes to dealing with heartache, I very much take after Mami. I swear there must be a gene for this, because we both approach heartache the same way: very logically and by suppressing our feelings to focus on how to solve our problems. Mami and I have always been doers, not dwellers. We do our best to take control while looking ahead, no matter how difficult the situation might be. I deal with adversity by analyzing, looking at all the possibilities, and relying on faith. While I wasn't able to witness it, I sense my mother acted accordingly that cataclysmic day.

Papi's body was released to our family late that evening. He went to work in the morning, a day like any other day, and by the time the sun set, he came home in a coffin. The autopsy report confirmed that he had suffocated from the weight of the machine on his chest. His lungs had collapsed. His external injuries were so severe that Mami was forced to hold a closed-casket wake the next day. Instead of celebrating Mother's Day, those who loved Papi paid their respects. He was buried in one of Mayagüez's private cemeteries, five hundred yards from where he and Mami lived.

Mami had lost the love of her life and was forced to go on the only way she knew how. After two weeks she returned to work. More than ever, she needed to hold down a job to support her family. Four weeks after Papi's passing, Mami gave birth to my sister, Jessica. By the time Mami turned twenty-one in August 1974, she had gone from a happily married mother of one to a widowed mother of two. But she was never alone, which helped ease the physical burden a bit. My maternal grandmother, Esperanza, my aunts, and my uncles helped care for our family. Mami's brother, Rafael, temporarily moved back to Puerto Rico from Manhattan. Her youngest sister, Ramona, who was only about ten years older than me, stopped by our house every day after school to help care for me and my sister.

Oddly, when my father passed, the dynamics between my mother's family and Papi's changed. I have always sensed that Mami must have had a falling-out with Candelaria, although she stayed in touch with Juan and Zara. Their relationship was always a rocky one and I can certainly vouch that Candelaria was far from easygoing. I have heard from family members that she tried to tell Mami what to do all the time, especially when it came to raising my sister and me. Maybe she thought Mom was not fit to raise us; maybe she was making Mami feel worse than she already did, given her circumstances; or perhaps there was a bigger secret and story behind it. The details of what truly happened between them are like a locked treasure at the bottom of the sea, the key well hidden. I have no other choice but to trust that Mami did what she had to do to overcome a terrible loss and provide us with the best upbringing possible.

Despite the animosity between my mother and grandmother, however, Mami never kept Jessica and me from seeing Candelaria. She would drop us off at Candelaria's house, not stay herself but insist that my dad's sister accompany us, which I found strange. Mami wanted us to see but not be alone with Candelaria. When I complained about going, she would say, "She is your dad's mom. You need to have a relationship with her." And she was right! But those visits were tortuous for me. I felt no warmth from her. Maybe she felt bitterness toward Mami. She was certainly not like most grandmas in Hispanic culture. She was not an integral part of our upbringing or a model of Christian piety in our lives. Candelaria always made me feel uncomfortable and uneasy. On the surface there was a palpable distance between us, but at the same time I felt a strange, unspoken sense of closeness. In snippets of conversations I would overhear between my relatives, I gathered there was much more to her than anyone wanted to openly talk about. All I know is that something caught my attention every time I visited her. Our energies seemed to collide and I had the eerie sense that there were other people in the house with us. Sadly, I don't recall the last time I ever saw her.

I was sixteen months old when Papi passed away. I have no

recollection of him—not his laughter or how his love made me feel. I don't remember the feel of his face or the smell of his skin or his touch or his tender kisses. I will always wonder what it feels like to have a dad, to have his love and presence in the physical world, to be a kid and go with him to the movies or to a father-and-daughter dance at school. When people around me lose their fathers, not only do I express my sympathy but I also say they are very lucky because they know how it feels to have a dad. I'll never know that feeling.

I've been told Papi deeply loved Mami and that he was a responsible husband, provider, and father. As a little girl, my logic was simple: *I have a mom who's a mom and a dad.* Mami attended events geared toward both parents, whether it was a Father's Day picnic at school, my graduation, or my senior prom, Mami escorted me so we didn't feel embarrassed or lacking in any way. I never played the victim because I didn't have a father the way some people do. I did, however, often wonder how different life would have been had I grown up with a father and whether Papi could see me and Jessica from heaven. I didn't know for sure back then, but I strongly suspected he was always looking over us!

I was very much kept in the dark about my father and how he passed. The conversations about him were kept short and followed the same script; no new information was ever offered. While recognizing it was a painful subject for all, there had to be more to the story. Shortly before Christmas when I was ten years old, I set out on my customary "scavenger hunt," rummaging through closets and boxes in search of the toys I knew my mom had cleverly tried to hide from us. Instead of toys I found a plastic bag with a zipper that I had not seen before. Curious, I opened it and rummaged through the items, pulling out a man's black leather wallet and front-page newspaper article about Papi's death. Until then I had no clue that his death had made the local news. I continued reading until my eyes fell on a graphic photo of the accident—an over-turned tractor and a man being carried away on a stretcher. In that instant Mami walked through the door and snatched the article away. "What are you doing?" she exclaimed, stunned to find me holding the truth in my hands at such a young age. I was startled into silence and didn't ask other questions. She put the wallet and newspaper story away and walked out.

I am not sure why there was so much mystery surrounding my father's death; I reasoned because it was so painful for my mom to remember. When I tried to bring it up, she would skillfully change the subject, a clear message that she refused to go there. At the time it was incredibly frustrating, but after having been through my share of emotional roller coasters as an adult, I get it—and I get her. She underwent a deeply traumatic experience, one that forty-something years later is still not easy for her to discuss. I can hear the emptiness in her voice when she tries. I feel her discomfort and I see the sadness in her eyes and her heart. Mami has always guarded her emotions and kept her feelings hidden deep in her heart.

Because my father's memory is wrapped in a veil of uncomfortable silence, I have always longed to connect via a psychic medium with my dad. Although I don't have memories of Papi beyond a few photos and cherished stories, I wholeheartedly believe that his spiritual presence has been with me since the day he died. I felt this more than ever on my wedding day. As a video of Mami and Papi's first dance from their wedding day filled the wall behind me during my first dance, my dad was not only dancing with me, I could feel his presence beside me.

I was also able to connect with Papi's Spirit through more tangible means.

A few days before Christmas 2016, when Mami, Jessica, Tío Rafael, and my niece and nephew were in town with Nick and I for the holidays, I received the best Christmas present ever. A very dear friend invited me to attend a private event with Theresa Caputo, star of the reality TV show *Long Island Medium*. As the date, January 5, 2017, approached, I prayed, over and over, *"Papi, please come through for me."*

Mami and Jessica were extremely skeptical and adamant nonbelievers in communicating with the dead, but before leaving home that afternoon I asked Mami, "If you had a chance to ask him a question, what would it be?" Without hesitation, she replied, "I want to know if he suffered."

The reading took place in a conference room at Theresa's book publisher's office. Theresa commanded the room with her big personality, signature puffy blond hair, and thick Long Island accent. After some small talk to the group to warm up the crowd, she said, "I should just stop talking, because I have all these spirits around me bugging me and talking to me at the same time." The room went quiet.

"Who has a deceased father in the room?" she asked. My heart stopped. Three of us raised our hands, two shyly and me without hesitation. Immediately drawn to a specific woman in the room, Theresa did the first reading with her. I was mesmerized by their exchange. Theresa then suddenly turned in my direction and planted herself right in front of me. "He's making a noise with something in his pocket," she said, putting her hands in her pockets to imitate the movement and sounds. "It's similar to the sound of loose change or keys." A chill ran down my spine. From the few stories that Mami had told me when I was growing up, I knew that every weeknight, when Papi came home from work and before he even opened the door, he would start rattling his keys as he entered. I would go crazy with delight, because it was my signal that Papi was home. He would then place them in my hands for me to play with. It was our very unique routine. I wanted to hear more from Papi.

"He is showing me that he banged his head, he's choking or can't breathe, something really tragic . . . Did he have a car crash?"

I nodded and explained that a freak accident caused his death.

"But he's telling me he didn't suffer as much as you all think. He didn't even know what was going on until he banged his head, felt he couldn't breathe, and then passed away." I stared at Theresa, stunned. Papi had just answered Mami's question, the one thing she wished to know for the past forty-three years.

"How do you connect with a black wallet?" she asked, adding that its contents are disintegrating; she said the photo and the driver's license were turning to dust, there were dollar bills shriveled as if burnt; all kept in a plastic bag.

Tears rolled down my cheeks as I thought about how I had found my dad's wallet when I was a child. I thought about the driver's license, faded with the laminate peeling, the washed-out photo of my mom when she was sixteen and the crumbling one-dollar bills. When the machine had crushed Papi, the diesel spilled out, soaking everything. The wallet in his pocket was drenched in diesel, which rotted its contents. No one knew about this except us in the family.

Theresa went on, asking about my connection to art. In

2015, I had founded a nonprofit foundation for which the key fund-raising concept is auctioning off artwork donated by mostly Hispanic artists. After a short pause, Theresa continued, "He is showing me the month of August and the number four." "August fourth is Mami's birthday," I replied, now almost speechless. "He's telling me he would give her a bouquet of red roses every year on her birthday as a symbol of his love for her." Theresa then said, "He is showing me a photo of himself. He is sitting on a couch. He says it was his favorite shirt."

I know that photo. It was taken in the late sixties during one of Papi's visits to his sister who lived in the Bronx and it is a photo I have always cherished. I always felt destined to live in New York City because of that photo. New York is a city my father loved with all his heart, and I am certain that every day when I walk the streets of this city I call home, he is here with me. I feel his presence all the time.

Theresa assured me that Papi was still involved with my life and with me every step of the way, guiding me and my foundation. She said he wanted me to know that he "feared you would not remember him or honor him, since you really didn't know him, and he wants to thank you for making him a part of your life all these years."

Theresa couldn't understand that message, but I did! These were not just standard lines she was throwing out. There was a deeper meaning. Throughout the reading I felt all sorts of emotions—joy, sorrow, loneliness, understanding, peace, grief—welling up inside me. I had validation, concrete proof from Papi that he was watching over me. This is what I yearned for, imagined, believed, felt, and hoped for my entire life.

And for the first time in my life I had an absolute sense of closure combined with an overwhelming rush of peace in my mind and heart—a feeling I had never felt before. After two decades of attempting to have a psychic medium connect me with Papi, I had finally achieved it. It was a life-changing experience.

But something else also happened that night. As Theresa was reading other people in the room before doing my own reading, I began to hear the same things she was telling them she was hearing. I felt I was connected to the same Spirit. Furthermore, I knew what she was going to say before she said it. I felt we were the same person: physically two different people but somehow connected by Spirit. One moment that stood out was the reading she gave to a babysitter of a toddler tragically drowned by his own mother in the bathtub. The toddler was showing Theresa how his brother played with toy trains in his bedroom. Just before she said this, an image of a train set popped into my head. At that moment, I realized: I was a psychic medium, just like Theresa.

The experience that evening made me realize my life was about to take on a whole new meaning. I had not only Papi's validation but evidence of my own gift.

On my ride home that night, I felt ecstatic. I let my emotions run where they wanted to and tried not to control them as I normally did. My heart was dancing to "Fly Me to the Moon" and I was singing one of my favorite operatic arias: Verdi's "Celeste Aida." I remember looking out the window of the Uber and repeatedly whispering under my breath, "Thank you, God, for allowing Papi to come through." I had also learned something about myself I would keep secret for now. I knew I had connected with the Spirit world, but where could I start learning about mediumship? How would I begin? Connecting with Papi was a sign that I needed to start thinking about serving others more seriously.

Before going to sleep that night, I pulled Mami aside and asked, "Did Dad give you anything on special occasions? Was there something specific he did to express his love?"

"He always gave me red roses," she replied almost immediately.

My heart skipped a beat and I smiled.

While I will always wonder what it is like to have a father in the physical world, I will never have to question ever again his presence in my life or his influence in my dreams or on this book.

The reading with Theresa made me realize that Spirit has always been a part of my life since my earliest memories. All mediums are born mediums. It's passed on from one generation to another, normally on the maternal side. On many occasions I saw shadows or silhouettes or signs, heard sounds, and often talked to "people" I could not touch or see. This has always been a part of me, and for forty-five years I have kept this secret from everyone, including my mom, sister, family members, and even my childhood best friends who thought they knew me well. I have had premonitions, such as the feeling that I was about to be involved in a car accident: I hit the brakes, and witnessed a crash not fifty yards in front of me. I feel other people's energy, and there have been times I could sense and smell illness. Close family members and friends who have passed have visited me in my dreams. When we lived in Sultana, a neighborhood of Mayagüez, our house was five hundred yards from a cemetery. Sometimes when we walked to the bowling alley, we walked by that cemetery, and the sensations overwhelmed me. Growing up, I did not like to visit my Papi's grave—not because I did not want to see him or be disrespectful, but because I was scared of other things I would feel. I have battled my entire life with anxiety as I suppressed my gift out of fear of rejection or being ridiculed. After all, who wants to be known as the girl who hears voices and sees the dead?

I nearly died when I was born. I was born again when I connected with one who had died.

3

When the Winds of Change Blow

You cannot swim for new horizons until you have
courage to lose sight of the shore.

—WILLIAM FAULKNER

The second house on the right at the end of a cul-de-sac on
Calle Marginal, facing the Carretera Número Dos, is the
first house I remember living in. Mami bought it a year after
Papi's death. Since his passing was due to a work-related accident, Mami received financial compensation that allowed
her to put a roof over our heads by making a down payment
on a house in the up-and-coming neighborhood of Sultana.
While I can't remember the day we moved in, the lovely
pastel-colored home remains one of the most important places
of my life. There was a big living room, a family room, a dining room, three bedrooms, two bathrooms, and a bright red
carpet that we hated so much that I can still picture it to this
day. The house was a new construction, in an upscale resi-
dential area—a step up—but what made it truly special was
the enormous backyard. It offered my sister and me countless
hours of entertainment on our own or with friends, as it had a
swing, a hammock, a roundabout, and lots of space. We even
had an aboveground pool from Sears! We also loved to spend

time in the *marquesina*, where we played bingo, and the cul-de-sac, where we roller-skated. In so many ways our home was the heart of the neighborhood, because we were always surrounded by friends, many of whom we still have. We never felt alone. When I think back on those years living in Sultana, I remember our home as the happiest place on earth: filled with joyful kids, screaming voices, and lots of laughter.

My sister and I had a very happy childhood; Mami made sure of it. Papi's tragic death did not turn our lives into a miserable, depressing existence. If life dealt Mami lemons, she made sure to make plenty of lemonade for us—and the entire island while she was at it. Never one to shrink before a challenge, she took on her new life without Papi with strength and determination. In the process, Mami taught us to do the same. We lived comfortably. We had what mattered most: love, food on the table, and a solid education. Vacations in Europe or stays at summer camp in the U.S., like some of the kids at school, were out of our league. Yet there was no pain or suffering in our house, no tears of sorrow, no sense of helplessness.

Life proceeded as normal until 1978 rolled around, when Mami decided we were going to move. I was five years old. I probably couldn't understand the enormity of what we were about to embark on.

"We need to pack up our things. We are moving to Los Angeles, and Tío Rafael is coming with us," she said matter-of-factly. I was too young to be consulted about this decision, but then again, Mami isn't a huge fan of discussing things. I think her desire to leave had a lot to do with her fearlessness and inclination to take risks to benefit herself and her children. My feeling is that Mami wanted so much more from life than what Mayagüez had to offer, and this pushed her to go out and explore the world. Not only was she still very young at the time, but so much had transpired since my sister and I had been born that she probably felt she could use a change of scenery, and what better place to reinvent oneself than sunny Los Angeles?

Tío Rafael is my fabulous openly gay uncle, the number one uncle in the world, and my role model on how to be an auntie to my nephew and niece. He is now in his late sixties and emigrated from Puerto Rico to the Bronx in the late 1960s to pursue the American dream. This was a well-known phenomenon in the history of Puerto Rico: the mass exodus in the 1950s to New York. He is just four years older than Mami, with dark skin like my grandfather Santiago. He spent twenty-eight years working on Wall Street and has lived in the same apartment in the Bronx, commuting every day on the 6 train through snow in the winter and heat waves in the summer. But when Papi died and Mami was in need, he put his budding career in finance and cool New York social life temporarily on hold for us. Tío Rafael left his colorful world in the Bronx to join ours in Puerto Rico and help Mami raise us.

Growing up, no one ever really told us Tío Rafael was gay. This was kept hush-hush. At the time there was still a profound stigma attached to homosexuality, but I got the hint when he brought his Welsh "roommate" Mr. Jones on vacation to our house.

Everyone in the family knows there is a uniquely special bond between Mami and my uncle—different from the relationship she has with her other siblings. He has always guided us, celebrated achievements and milestones with us, and dried our tears when a steady hand was needed.

Tío Rafael holds the title as the most stable male figure in my life. He has always been present, regardless of distance, to support my mother and us in whatever ways we needed. Although it was never officially said, he has always taken on the father-figure role in our family. Not surprisingly, he was the one to give me away at my wedding. Many years later I found out that Tío Rafael helped finance part of our private Catholic schooling. And when Tío Rafael eventually moved back to New York to resume his career and pursue his dreams, he never stopped looking after us.

As a teenager, while flipping through *Vogue* and *Teen Beat* magazines, I would pine over the fashionable dresses from designers sold at New York department stores, rip out specific pages, and carefully circle the dresses that made my heart swoon. I would mail Tío Rafael the earmarked pages and, sure enough, a couple weeks later I would receive one of them in the mail. I have always had a connection with fashion, not from a materialistic perspective, but as a means of personal expression and way to stand out in a crowd—ultimately, a form of art. The dresses were not so much about satisfying my capricious teenage desires as wearing a look that would set me apart from everyone else. I was different. I wanted that to be known. I never imitated anyone. If I had told him I wanted the moon on a string, he would have responded, without hesitation: "Hold on, I'll be right back!"

So, the moment Mami mentioned her crazy idea about moving to Los Angeles, Tío Rafael knew he had no choice but to join us. And that's how we were off to a place where we knew nobody, but we felt the promise of a new beginning.

The day we landed at LAX, I felt like we had landed on a different planet. I was five years old. It was my first time outside Puerto Rico. Heck, it was my first time riding on an airplane and my first time in a place where everyone else spoke another language. As a kid, of course, I quickly fell in love with that feeling of newness and adventure. To this day it's one of the things I love most about traveling. I get a kind of high when going somewhere for the first time to explore different cultures, languages, and food. It's why traveling to new places features high up on the life list Nick and I compiled that night at Dylan Prime in Tribeca.

As we pulled out of the airport in the cab that would take us to our temporary home at a Holiday Inn, I was the kid with her head sticking out of the window, taking in all the sights, including the intertwining highways and never-ending traffic. I remember it took us a long time to get to our hotel, but with every stop sign and traffic light I gazed out the window and absorbed it all: the pristine blue skies, the wide streets and tidy sidewalks, and of course the renowned golden arches: McDonald's. As we drove around the City of Angels, I was mesmerized by just how absolutely new and clean everything looked—just like in the movies. What caught my eye the most? That everyone had new cars, which was vastly different from Puerto Rico.

Within days of arriving, Mami and Tío Rafael got to work finding us a more permanent place to live. But every time they applied for an apartment in the neighborhoods where we wanted to live—Los Feliz and Hollywood—our applications were rejected. The reason? Apparently, landlords didn't like having children under five in their apartment complexes.

However, I have always sensed the real reason was that none of these landlords wanted Hispanics in their buildings. Tío Rafael spoke fluent English, but none of us girls did. After several tries, my mom realized Los Angeles wasn't for us, and so she set her sights on another city: San Francisco. Unlike Los Angeles, she knew one person in San Francisco, a friend of a friend. However, almost as soon as we got there, Mami realized it wasn't what she had in mind for us either. Anyone else might have packed up and gone home at that point, accepting that things just weren't working out, that they weren't meant to be, but not Mami. She was determined. She kept trying and trying and would not give up. She called Teresa, one of her best childhood friends, who lived in San Antonio, Texas, in search of a friendly voice and advice. Teresa encouraged Mami to move to San Antonio.

After two months of attempting to make California work, the four of us moved to Texas. Following a brief stint at a hotel in the River Walk area of San Antonio, Mami managed to rent an apartment in the same complex as Teresa. She furnished the apartment and enrolled us in school, and so our Texan adventure began.

Growing up in Puerto Rico, I had lived in a close-knit Puerto Rican community. My family was Puerto Rican, my neighbors were Puerto Rican, my friends were Puerto Rican. In Los Angeles, I could not help but notice the diversity. I had never seen or met anyone from Asia for example, but as we drove and walked around the city, I became aware of people who looked different from me. I was fascinated. San Antonio was very different again. The city has a large Mexican population, and Mexican culture is everywhere. Well, Texas was part of Mexico once!

Our apartment in San Antonio was located in a complex that was home to middle-income families. It had all sorts of upscale amenities that we didn't have in Puerto Rico: central heating and air-conditioning, a gym, beautifully manicured gardens, and a large in-ground swimming pool. Whoa!

Being kids, we frequented the pool almost every single day,

yet every time I walked to the edge of the deep end, longing to jump in and swim with my new friends from the apartment complex, Mami would pull me back to the shallow end and forbid me from ever trying that again because I didn't know how to swim. That was all I needed to hear for my determination to kick in, and to this day, if someone says I can't do something, I take it on as a challenge to prove them wrong.

Sure enough, the first streak of my fearless personality burst onto the scene a few weeks later on a hot, sunny afternoon. Mami was deep in conversation with one of our neighbors. It was my chance to finally swim in the deep end like the rest of my friends. Sprinting swiftly over to the deep end of the pool, I glanced back and realized my great escape had worked. My mother was still engrossed in her conversation and my absence had gone undetected. Without hesitation, I leaped into the water. No one saw me do it until they heard the splash. At long last I fulfilled what I had been gunning to do for weeks on end.

Of course, any sense of accomplishment was quickly usurped by a life-threatening moment. My first recollection was a trail of bubbles as I tried to breathe but inhaled water. I sank farther and farther down toward the bottom of the pool. Then, just as fast, I saw that someone had jumped in after me. It was Mami. Her hands desperately flailing in the water, she tried to reach and save me—but instead of pulling me up she was actually sinking farther into the depths of the pool. She didn't know how to swim either! Then, as my panic kicked in, I saw a *third* person jump into the pool who pulled both of us out of the water in a matter of seconds! Turns out, it was our neighbor Wayne: I have never forgotten his name or face. He was a Navy SEAL, tall and strong. He was our savior.

The next thing I remember was spitting out water as Wayne compressed my belly and the muffled siren of an ambulance wailing in the distance. The paramedics arrived and checked us out. Mami and I turned out to be fine, but the lesson had been learned: we needed swimming lessons *pronto*.

Looking back, I was gutsy. How did I dare to jump? I could have sworn a voice told me to. This was my second brush with death. I realized I was meant to be in the world, that it wasn't my time to leave just yet, and I'd better learn how to swim.

Eventually our happy time in the Lone Star State came to an end. Only seven months after leaving our enchanted island, Mami decided to go back home to Puerto Rico. We had our family and our lives there, after all. Mami promptly got to work selling what furniture she could, packing up the rest of our belongings, and breaking the lease. Our life on the mainland had come to an end.

❧

When we got back to Mayagüez, we didn't exactly pick up where we had left off. Tío Rafael wanted to stay in the States, so we said our goodbyes at the San Antonio airport and he went back to his New York life. Since Mami had rented out our home in Sultana when we moved to California, we had to rent another house. Mami picked a white two-story house with tiles and no red carpet. The house sat across from a sugarcane plantation in Barrio Ballajá in Cabo Rojo, a city near Mayagüez. We spent a year there, but by the time I was eight years old we moved back to our home in Sultana once the tenant's lease had come to an end.

Before we left for Los Angeles, Mami had enrolled me in prekindergarten at Colegio Presbiteriano. Once I reached kindergarten, my teacher alerted my mom that I tended to get bored and chitchat. Either I was understimulated or a budding chatterbox or, as I've since learned, a little of both! I underwent a number of intelligence and behavioral assessment tests to determine how to handle my case.

While most of the kids in my class were still learning how to read and write, I was already capable of doing so on my own. I vividly remember the psychologist who conducted the evaluation. I sat at a wooden square table with children's chairs, the abacus, and all these colorful toys. There were also cards and memory games. I can remember telling the psychologist that his questions were boring. It was determined that my social, organizational, and emotional skills, along with my IQ, merited skipping me to first grade.

Mami had the last word. She agreed.

During the end of my first semester in first grade, a school administrator suggested that I skip to second grade, but Mami decided; jumping up one grade was enough. She didn't want to put me in a situation where I was so much younger than everyone else in my class. More importantly, she didn't want me to feel awkward or inadequate among my classmates. Her biggest concern was that skipping me again would set me up to fail. I would be growing up too fast. She wanted me to be successful. Regardless, I remained the youngest in my class during the rest of my elementary and high school years.

Before we left for our adventures on the mainland, my mother started dating a gentleman named Fidel. Along with Tío Rafael, Fidel has been an important male father figure in my life. Fidel is unconventional: a criminal defense and family law attorney, a socialist who despite his self-made wealth lives life frugally. He is an avid reader, an authority on many subjects, blessed with an inquisitive and challenging mind. He is generous and always a source of advice and comfort for me. Fidel doesn't fit into one of society's ready-made boxes.

Spending time at Fidel's countryside house surrounded by thirty-six acres of land, tucked in the mountainous area of Mayagüez, twenty minutes of windy roads away from Sultana, was a major part of my upbringing. I interacted with nature, from being around animals—cows, hens, chickens, and horses—to eating real organic food picked straight from the land. However, I have never been a big animal person: I would occasionally pat the horses but never milked a cow! On the other hand, my sister loved all of it. Some of my favorite memories are when we, as a family, picked oranges and *plátanos* straight from the trees, and dug potatoes, yuca, *ñames*, and *yautías* from the ground.

After spending the entire day in the countryside, we would bring home our bounty. Mami would then transform our gatherings into delicious and healthy meals. Mami has always been an excellent cook. I grew up eating healthfully and supporting sustainable living long before the current trend—and we didn't even know it!

Fidel is the person who introduced me to some of the world's most important works of literature. To call him a voracious reader is an understatement and disservice, because it's not just that he reads a lot of books but that he can have the most intelligent discussions, debates, and conversations of anyone I've ever known. He hasn't traveled the world and doesn't care to, but he knows more about the history, the culture, and the people of so many countries without having ever been there. The newspaper is more important to him than religion or food. During my teenage years I sat with him to talk about authors like Gabriel García Márquez,

Gabriela Mistral, Julia de Burgos, Miguel de Cervantes, Mario Vargas Llosa, Isabel Allende, Pablo Neruda, and Mario Benedetti to name a few. We would discuss the books, read our favorite passages, and talk about what we thought the author wanted to convey. He knew how to guide me in the discussion, asking the right questions, yet never making me feel like he was actually *teaching* me something; he allowed me to explore my own ideas freely regardless of whether they were "right" or "wrong." I realize now he assigned me to read those books with a purpose: to make me a well-rounded young lady.

Although Fidel still lives in Puerto Rico, and I haven't seen him since 2013, we are still in touch. The first phone call I made after obtaining my book deal was to Fidel. I have never seen him cry, but I suspected once we hung up he shed tears of happiness for me.

Every time I receive one of his letters, always at the most pivotal moments in my life, I get super excited, because his words are poetry. I keep them by my bedside and read them often to remind myself of him.

❧

Before I finished sixth grade, Mami decided that it was time to move again, and this time it wasn't on a whim: she had a two-year plan. The goal was for Jessica and me to really learn English. She wanted us to study the language to fully master life in the United States before we headed off to college. It was another tool for a better future—and she was right. I can't imagine what my life would be like if I hadn't had those years to truly solidify my command of the English language and American culture. But this time we didn't head back to sunny California or beautiful Texas. This time my mother moved us to

Jersey City. It wasn't a random choice, though: we had traveled to New York the previous two summers to visit my aunts and uncles. My mom was happy to be closer to her siblings, and Jersey City was just a ferry ride away from Manhattan.

At the time, Abuela Esperanza, my mom's mother, was living half of the time in Puerto Rico and the other half in the Bronx. Her husband, Abuelo Santiago, had suffered a stroke almost twenty years earlier; my grandmother, who had been by his side and tending to his every need since the day they were married, suddenly found herself alone when he died from a heart attack in 1982. That was when Abuela Esperanza moved in with Mami's oldest sister, Gabriela, in the Bronx. But like my mother, far from letting the death of her husband get her down, Abuela Esperanza tackled life head-on and began to flourish in ways we had never seen. She started living on her own terms, coming and going as she pleased with no one to take care of. But she still needed someone to care for her and look after her. So when we decided to move to Jersey City in the summer of 1984, it was only natural for Abuela Esperanza to move in with us and to give Gabriela a break from being her caretaker.

For many American families, it might sound like a nightmare to have to live with your grandmother, but in our Latin culture it's absolutely normal and a complete joy: grandmothers are in their grandchildren's life all the time, and they help care for the kids. The *abuelas* are the family matriarchs. For me it was a wonderful gift to have three generations living under the same roof.

One of Mami's half brothers, Julio—Santiago had four children from a previous marriage—worked as the superintendent of a large two-hundred-unit Tudor-style building on

Fairview Avenue between Bergen Avenue and John F. Kennedy Boulevard, and he was able to get us a rental there at a reasonable price. Mami enrolled us at Saint Aloysius Elementary Academy, a Catholic school located just a few blocks away from our apartment, but the initial experience was far from what I could have ever imagined. During the summer before school started, we hung out with our cousins in the neighborhood, and they introduced us to their friends. Although my sister and I already spoke some English, that summer we learned the language we were really going to need to get by in our new life: street English. We had to learn all the local slang: *Guido* meant Italian American; *Chicano* meant Mexican American; *exit* wasn't a means of leaving somewhere, it was were you lived; and *the shore* meant the beach. We felt like we were adapting perfectly, but the true shock came on the first day of school at Saint Aloysius. Back home in Mayagüez, I took great pride in being a straight-A student, so when I started seventh grade as an ESL (English as a second language) student in a system that was foreign to me, I felt "less than." I was used to being three steps ahead of everyone else. Now I was relegated to the ESL group, made up exclusively of children who couldn't communicate in English. Despite the fact that I *thought* I already spoke English, my teacher's assessment was that I was far from fluent. I went from being at the top of my class to the lowest part of the grade totem pole, and I was not having it. Upset and somewhat lost, it took me a while to find my place in this new world. True to myself, I never let it get the better of me. I set out to prove to everyone at this new school—and to myself—that my academic prowess was still top-notch; nothing was going to stop me from being the kind of student that I was back home.

I'll never forget one of those first days at school when my English teacher, with her long and very blond hair and heavy Jersey accent, asked, "Who wants to read this sentence?" Used to participating in school and being an extrovert, I threw my hand up in the air and suddenly became extremely self-conscious as my classmates turned to me in bewilderment and exchanged mocking glances as if I were some sort of alien that couldn't possibly know how to read. But as soon as I opened my mouth, they were shocked to learn that even though I had a thick accent, I actually could read and speak English. Even though they were the ones who had the misconception, for some reason I felt terribly embarrassed and ashamed: it had never occurred to me that the other children could see me as inferior to them in some way. A few classmates approached me after class to say they never knew I really spoke English, and from that point on I began to make friendships in the class. I had proven them wrong, but either way it was a reality check. At school for years to come, I was often one of only a handful of Hispanics among my classmates. Yes, I was different, and I couldn't yet converse as well as my classmates did, but I didn't allow that to stop me from being me or cause me to retreat or hide. In fact, it had quite the contrary effect on me: the less people expected from me, the more I wanted to show them they were wrong. It's a feeling I've had my entire life.

If seventh grade was the year in which I had to make new friends and adapt to life in the United States, eighth grade was the year I became a full-fledged American teenager. Having graduated from the ESL group, that year I became a part of the track team, started to get good grades, found a group of friends, and was even experiencing my first case of puppy love. Yes, Jersey City was the scene of my very first kiss. The pucker in question had light brown eyes, light brown hair, and olive skin. He was Italian American; his name was Tony (of course), and together we were like a pair straight out of *West Side Story*. He went to the local public school with my cousin Zelda. Once or twice per week we would meet up in the alley behind the school building to make out. All we did was kiss! Of course, my mother didn't have the slightest idea of the shenanigans I was up to.

It's amazing what confidence and self-esteem can do! I went from being apprehensive about Jersey living to truly loving school. Jersey City gave us a home and security, but my heart wasn't into Jersey City. What I can say is that those were the years when I fell deeply in love with Manhattan.

My sister, my mother, and I would often go into the city to visit the sights and all that Manhattan offered. I'll never forget the first time I ever attended a live concert without parental supervision. My sister, cousin Zelda, and I got tickets to see Menudo, the Puerto Rican boy band that was taking the world by storm. Like all teenage girls at the time, I beyond *loved* Menudo. My room was filled with teen pop Menudo posters and memorabilia. The cherry on the top was that we had been given permission to go into the city on our own. We took the PATH from Journal Square to Manhattan. I felt like a grown-up. At Thirty-Fourth Street we took the subway uptown to Radio City Music Hall. It was raining that day. I vividly remember leaving the subway station at rush hour, walking onto a crowded Manhattan street, zigzagging around people, and taking cover under a canopy of strangers' umbrellas. Being surrounded by a sea of people of all ages, walks of life, and appearances—men dressed in suits with shiny shoes, women in their skirts and coats with sneakers rushing to get somewhere—I truly couldn't get enough of it. I couldn't help but absorb the vibrant energy and adrenaline rush. I was in awe of what was unfolding before my eyes, unaware that a couple of decades later that very city would be my permanent home. I've always visualized myself in Manhattan, because in many ways it is the center of the world: a melting pot of people and cultures. Early on, while I was still living in Puerto Rico, I realized that I am a city girl. After all, Mayagüez is a city and had already given me a taste of urban living.

Our time in Jersey City was very happy, surrounded by my maternal grandma, uncles, aunt, cousins, and many friends. But as we all know, nothing lasts forever. When I was halfway through eighth grade, after the midterm exams, Mami sat my sister and me down after dinner to announce that at the end of the school year we would be heading back to Puerto Rico. I thought she had forgotten about it or would change her mind, since we were happy, we were doing well, and we had our family close by. Even though we knew we were only supposed to stay for two years, we were shocked when she gave us the news. Adapting to our new lives in Jersey City hadn't been a slam dunk, yet here we were, finally in full swing with our school, classmates, and extracurricular activities, and now we had to up and leave again? We were fuming. "I told you it would only be two years," she said. "I don't want you to do high school here."

I think one of the real reasons for our sudden departure was that Mami had been shocked earlier that semester when my school informed all the eighth-grade parents that my fourteen-year-old classmate Lauren was pregnant. We were surprised as well but didn't make too much of it. Mami, however, had very clear goals and priorities in mind for us girls, and getting pregnant at fourteen was definitely not what she envisioned for her daughters. In our traditional Hispanic culture, girls aren't supposed to have sex before getting married, much less get pregnant. If so, God would punish you. My mom worried that if we hung around with those who had such poor values, we might lose our way. Even though there might have been similar situations or risks in Puerto Rico, I imagine that, to a certain extent, Mami felt like she could handle them, since we would be surrounded by a culture she knew well.

What Mami also likely didn't know but suspected was that this was also the year that I was first exposed to drugs. I never did them, but it was the first time I became aware of their existence and heard about people who used them in my school. My mom had sent us to a Catholic school because she liked that we were taught morals and strict discipline, but little did she know that everything she wanted to protect us from was also happening under our noses.

No matter how much I begged her to let us stay in Jersey City, Mami's decision was final. Her decisions were always final: we were going home. Once her mind was made up, there was no turning back. Reluctantly we once again packed up all of our belongings, said goodbye to our friends in the United States, and flew back to Puerto Rico to reacquaint ourselves with the lives we had left behind.

I was now thirteen going on fourteen, a full-fledged teenager about to start high school. At that age it's all about extremes; things are either great and fantastic and unbelievable, or they are the worst: life sucks. My feelings at the time were no exception; the transition back to Puerto Rico felt like torture. I was unhappy, and, unlike in Jersey City, where I liked going to school and participating in all sorts of social and extracurricular activities, the school in Cabo Rojo made me nervous and unsettled. The school premises were not as fancy as Saint Aloysius, and the uniforms were horrific, like Pepto-Bismol. In fact, everyone in the entire island knew the ugly Pepto uniforms—sleeveless blazer to the hips, hideous and unflattering polyester A-line skirts—worn by the girls in Cabo Rojo. I also had to put plans of getting into a top university in the U.S. aside. For me, it was taking three steps back and going back into a box. It didn't help that I had preconceived notions about my new classmates: they would be rich, conceited, and arrogant kids from the more affluent families in Cabo Rojo. But by the second month of school I started to make some friends. I made the best of it—although, come to think of it, I never really had a choice. Mami had made that choice for me, as most parents do. My mother was the authority in our lives, so I had to make it work without questioning her.

Even though at times it was very difficult to uproot ourselves so often, moving throughout my childhood taught me how to adapt to different environments, how to let go of loved ones, how to survive any change thrown my way, how to befriend new classmates, and how to persevere no matter the circumstances. The experiences in Los Angeles, Texas, Jersey City, and back home in Puerto Rico taught me something else: to admire my mother for her courage and conviction to do the right thing for her children. Those same traits are mine as well.

This is the period where I began to dip my toes into womanhood, and I started observing my mother as a female role model. She is a beautiful woman who turned heads whenever she walked into a room. She was actually so attractive that my elementary and high school classmates didn't miss a chance to check her out! Boys in my sixth grade and high school classes would say, "*¡Hola, Doña Paola!*" with much respect, while they took her in from head to toe.

Mami takes great pride in her appearance: she dresses and accessorizes well and taught me the importance of always looking good, not leaving your house without makeup, and washing your face every night. I've used eye cream since I was sixteen years old. As a teenager, I happened to be the same shoe size as Mami, so the first pair of heels I ever wore for one of my first high school parties were hers: a killer pair of Charles Jourdan black patent pumps from La Favorita, a shoe store known for importing all the top styles, including from Parisian and Spanish shoe designers. Slipping my feet into those pumps marked my life.

Through my mom's *Vanidades* and *¡Hola!* magazines, not only did I learn everything there is to know about European royalty, I also discovered Oscar de la Renta, one of her favorite designers, and then slowly started finding my own style and my own favorites, including the iconic Karl Lagerfeld and Chanel. I really looked up to my mom when it came to dressing up; I followed in her footsteps, learning how to look good, how to be well put together, accessorize, and truly relish the process. Even to this day, when she's visiting, if she happens to catch me stepping out of the apartment in my sweats with no makeup and my hair in a bun, she freaks out. "At least put some powder on, *nena*, and while you're at it, some eyeliner and powder. And do your eyebrows: you can't go out looking like that!" When she knows I have an upcoming doctor's appointment, her first question is not about how I'm feeling or whether I'm nervous or what type of checkup I'm getting. No, her first question is, "Are you wearing a fresh pair of underwear?" And if I have to go to the hospital for any reason, she'll insist I pack a brand-new pair of pajamas. A huge part of Hispanic culture is that we've got to keep up our appearances no matter how awful we may feel. Outward beauty is often seen as a sign of internal health, well-being, and morality. And while in other cultures this may seem superficial or superfluous, life has taught me that there is some truth to it. My mother's insistence on always looking good, always putting your best face forward, has a lot to do with the way you tackle the challenges that life throws your way. When you know you look good, you feel confident. And confidence is the most important quality when it comes to facing any situation you might find yourself in.

When I turned seventeen, I registered at the Universidad de Puerto Rico, Mayagüez campus. Interestingly, I decided to major in biology, following my teenage dream of becoming a doctor. More specifically I wanted to be a pathologist, the person that does autopsies! Given what I know now about my health and the different illnesses that have plagued me throughout my life, who knows what would have become of me if I had studied to be a doctor. However, I went from being a top-tier student in high school to suddenly getting Ds and Fs during my first semester in college. I even failed calculus! The sudden freedom and wide array of options before me threw me for a loop. I was a seventeen-year-old college freshman who went from having a regimented Catholic school routine with a great emphasis on discipline, rules, and strict guidelines to being able to do pretty much whatever I wanted for the first time in my life. I was like a kid in a candy store. Honestly, I probably enjoyed it a little too much, as my grades clearly reflected.

When Mami found out I had failed calculus, she looked

me straight in the eyes and said, "I will help you pay for the next semester, but after that, you are on your own." She wasn't going to continue sacrificing herself to pay for my party time with the Mu Alpha Phi sorority. Since I knew her word was gold, I pulled myself together and got my first job at Novus, the new upscale shoe shop in town, owned by the Castellón family, who also owned La Favorita. My reasoning: might as well work with a product that I love.

The dip in grades was actually not all related to having too much of a good time. The reality was that my major also wasn't singing to me the way I had imagined. I was lost. No one actually sat me down to think about what it was I actually wanted to do with my life and what I might be good at. All I was going on were my hopes and dreams and not the reality of who I was. As I searched in my heart to find what would be my new major, I realized I had always had a strong interest in politics, so I switched my major to political science. My true calling would arrive many years later, once I was out fending for myself in the real world.

During my second year of college, when I was eighteen, I had my first serious boyfriend, Pablo. We met in college. He was four years older than I was and taking a little longer than he should have to graduate. He showed me the excitement of first love and gave me my first heartbreak. It ended after two years, with him dumping me for an older girl. Although he never said it, I sensed not agreeing to have sex with him was the reason for our breakup. Remember, I was raised Catholic and infused with Catholic guilt. I was taught that sex before marriage led to God punishing you and sending you straight to hell. That put the fear of God in me. No matter how much I liked Pablo, I was not ready to deal with God's wrath just to please my boyfriend. I was naïve and didn't realize sex could be such an important factor in the quest for love.

I was of course devastated. My family was upset, too, because they really liked Pablo. He spent Christmas with my family, his parents would visit our house, and my family trusted him. Even my mother trusted him enough to allow me to go out on dates with him until midnight. Remember, I was living at home during my time in college, and she would still monitor my movements: I had to be home by midnight or would turn into a pumpkin! Although Mayagüez is the fourth-largest city in Puerto Rico, it is still a relatively small place. One of the hardest aspects of my breakup with Pablo was that I would bump into him at sorority and fraternity events and at concerts, and sometimes I would see him around town with the girl he had left me for.

However, as time went by, the wound started to heal, and one day many months later Pablo invited me to lunch—a lunch that later ended up at his house and in his bed. I was nineteen, a few weeks shy of turning twenty, and had lost my virginity to my first love. I somehow knew deep down that he would be the first person I would be intimate with. He had been a very important part of my life for two years. But as I left his house, I knew I did not want to get back together with him. This was the closing of a chapter. Yet I was wracked with Catholic guilt. *Is my face going to show what I just did? Can people tell by just looking at me? Will my mom know?* I wanted to rush to my journal and write all about it, but I was scared that someone might find it and read it. It was a risk I wasn't willing to take. If my mom found out, she would kill him first and then kill me!

One of the few people I confided in was Rosa, one of my

best friends, whom I had met back in ninth grade. Rosa had moved to California with her family after completing ninth grade, and although we didn't see each other, we kept in touch through letters and phone calls. In the summer of 1994, Rosa visited Puerto Rico, and I was thrilled to hang out with her. Aware that I had not had another boyfriend after Pablo, she turned to me with a delightful smirk and said, "Why don't you come with me to California this summer? You need a change of scenery and men! I'll pay for your ticket." At first I thought I couldn't possibly accept, but the more I thought about it, the more I liked the idea. Spending time in California, away from my family and with one of my best friends? What was there not to like?

Rosa and I spent most of August in California, and by the time I boarded the plane to go back home, I had made up my mind to live life on my own terms.

"Mami, at the end of this semester, I'm moving to California," I said the very evening I got back from my trip. We were sitting at the dining room table after finishing our dinner.

"What?" Mami asked emphatically. "Are you crazy?"

Mami had a look of disbelief on her face, her eyes fixed on mine. Before I could even respond to her question, she drenched me with all the reasons I couldn't follow through with such a crazy plan: why I needed to stay in college, why it was a bad idea to move without a degree in hand, why I was still too young to leave Puerto Rico. Fidel also intervened to walk me off the ledge. But my mind was made up. The time had come for me to set out and find my own life and to claim my independence. Up until then I had always lived at home with my mother and sister. I respected Mami and listened to her advice, but I knew deep in my heart that my moment had come. I also wanted to free my mother from all those years of sacrifice and care and learn how to fend for myself. The time had come to finally spread my wings and let my free spirit take flight. I didn't feel that I belonged; I wanted more, I dreamed of so much more, including letting my spirit run wild.

In September, as I planned my journey to a new life, I was ambushed with debilitating stomach and digestive issues. I attributed it to exam stress. I was not going to let it get in the way of uprooting my life at the end of the year. The sudden, sharp upper-stomach pain, nausea, and vomiting became worse, more intense, and reached the point where I couldn't eat. In late October Mami finally decided to make an appointment with my primary care doctor, and none too soon: my gallbladder, the small, hollow organ where bile is stored before it is released into the small intestine for digestion, had a serious infection and was full of gallstones. I needed to undergo immediate surgery before it ruptured. I was alarmed by the diagnosis, but the doctor reassured me and explained that there was nothing to worry about. It was a fairly common ailment and the solution was to remove the whole organ.

Even after I received the diagnosis, I quit my shoe store job as planned, bought the airline ticket to California, and proceeded with my escape plan. I was due to fly to California on Thursday, December 15, 1994. The idea that this surgery could cause me to put my dream on pause was unfathomable. I looked the surgeon straight in the eye and said, "You can operate as long as you can guarantee I will be ready to catch my flight to California. I can't change it, and I am moving no matter what." Nothing was going to stop me . . . not even a health derailment.

4

Coloring Outside the Lines

We must accept finite disappointment,
but we must never lose infinite hope.
—MARTIN LUTHER KING JR.

On December 13, 1994, two days before moving to Irvine, California, I had my gallbladder surgery stitches removed. Because the bile stored in the gallbladder is designed to help digest fatty and spicy foods like peppers, the doctor advised me to permanently stay away from such foods. I took note, did everything he said to speed up my recovery, and was on my way to what I envisioned was going to be an exciting new chapter in my life. The surgery seemed like a hiccup in the days before my departure.

I couldn't wait to leave. I was leaving my family, the comfort of home, my mom's cooking, my friends—all for the hope of a fresh start in California. I had done very little to prepare for that future, to be honest. I hadn't even researched colleges or where to apply for a job. I planned to arrive at Rosa's college apartment just as I was. Somehow everything would work out.

I realize now how irresponsible the move was. But I was eager to make a change. That was foremost in my mind.

The time I spent with Rosa over the summer in California made me realize a future in Puerto Rico wasn't for me. Being on my own and away from my family allowed me to see things differently, take a step back, and analyze what was really going on with my life and where I wanted to head. I no longer wanted to complete my degree at Universidad de Puerto Rico. I didn't want to follow the path of so many of my friends who were in long-term relationships, planning to get married and have children. I couldn't see myself getting hitched as a main goal in life, and certainly not at my age. As I thought about the women I knew, I had a recurring thought: *I don't want this life for me right now. This is not me. I feel suffocated. I cannot be myself.* As time went by, my rejection of everything that surrounded me became almost visceral. I simply *had* to leave. I wasn't quite sure what I wanted yet, but I was clear that the conventional Latina box closing in on me at home was too restraining and limiting for my personality. I was not destined to get married, be a housewife, and bear children before I had spread my wings, traveled the world, pursued a career, and found my purpose. The summer with Rosa opened my eyes to the fact that there was more to life than the usual script of marriage and kids. I saw a new world full of possibilities, new friends, and *boom!*—it hit me like a ton of bricks: Los Angeles and Orange County, California, were my oyster. I am convinced that in life there are no coincidences. In the same way I was confident New York City was in the stars for me, Los Angeles was also meant to be an important stop in my journey—one that Mami had introduced me to years before and that I had never fully forgotten.

California represented a wealth of opportunities all within my reach, and after spending time there I knew that what I most desired was not to find a husband but to follow my own voice. If that meant coloring outside the socially conventional lines, so be it.

Many friends and family thought I was nuts to up and leave like that. They warned me that I would get homesick and even bet that I would be crawling back home in no time. But as they laughed and made jokes, my inner voice told me to keep calm and carry on. I was going away. I had no intention of coming back. I was going to build my legend and carve my very own destiny. My life was in my hands.

That Thursday, December 15, 1994, my mother and Fidel took me to the Mayagüez airport with my friend Linda who wanted to spend the holidays with Rosa and me. It was a bittersweet goodbye: my mother hugged me tightly and told me to take care of myself, while I tried to hide my tears behind my sunglasses. I could sense that my mom was in pain, but she would never show it or tell me. Her silence gave it away. I waved my last goodbyes from the tarmac and boarded the small-engine plane for the thirty-minute flight to San Juan. There I waited for two hours before boarding the plane that would take me to LAX.

I settled into my seat, fastened my seat belt—being cautious of the incisions in my belly—and looked outside my window to see the blue turquoise Mar Caribe and El Morro. As the plane took off, that small, still voice inside of me—call it instinct or the familiar, comforting reassurance of my guardian angels—gently whispered: *Don't worry. Do not fear. This is your path.* I can say that I never, ever looked back. Of course, I made lots of mistakes and I hit hard times, but I have not even once regretted this decision, because it launched me on a path I knew I always wanted.

I set foot in Rosa and her college roommates' apartment in Irvine, California, with two suitcases and eight hundred dollars in the bank. I went from comfortably living at home with Mami to sharing a three-bedroom apartment with five women. For the first time in my life, I was on my own. I had lived in a traditional Hispanic home where my mother took care of everything, where I had chores and was expected to help around the house, but there were many things I never had to even think of, which included washing my own clothes! When I was shown my bedroom, I glanced over to the one lonely bed in the corner, which quickly brought me down to my new reality: I would have to share that bed with one of my new roommates until I managed to buy my own twin mattress. When I finally did, it was hardly the height of luxury. But it allowed me to claim my own corner of the room, and that felt like claiming my own small corner of the world.

My roommates were kind and welcoming. Regardless of the crowded living setup, I was thrilled to be in a diverse and independent environment, my first "college life" experience. Compared to my previous situation, it was the difference between night and day. Living under the same roof as these girls, I realized that sex didn't have to be taboo. On the contrary, in my new environment, sex talk was a healthy, encouraged conversation.

One of my roommates, Mary, had a room all to herself and was so sexually active that there were always condom wrappers scattered across her bedroom floor. If my mom had seen that place with her own eyes, she would've been horrified, although I'll admit it was quite the eye-opener for me too. I quickly learned that sex wasn't something to fear; it was normal and meant to be enjoyed when practiced safely.

As the culture shock slowly wore off, it was time to find a job. The fastest way for me to do that was to trade on my previous experience working as a sales assistant. I found two jobs, one at a women's apparel boutique and another at a women's and men's clothing store. With the money I was able to make from these two jobs, I could pay my rent and expenses. Because I wasn't able to afford a car yet, Rosa or one of my colleagues at work would occasionally give me a lift to work. But for the most part I used public transportation and my own two legs—more specifically, two buses and a ten-minute walk to and from the bus stop at each end. This meant leaving the house two hours before my scheduled start time to avoid being late. But I didn't care. I was willing to do whatever it took to make this new life work. I often dreamed of the life I was going to build for myself and all the things I was going to do. I wanted to travel, to see the museums of Florence, the cafés of Paris, and the opera in New York. I wrote it all down in journals. These plans and dreams were what got me through some difficult times, even when I wasn't sure what was going to come next.

Rosa and I were eventually able to move out of the over-crowded apartment and into a one-bedroom located in front of South Coast Plaza in Costa Mesa. One bedroom and two twin beds—a total luxury after my crash-course experience in roommate living. I was twenty-two, I had my own place, albeit shared with Rosa, and steady employment that paid the monthly bills. I was still adjusting to my new life and discovering the path I would ultimately follow.

I was young and eager to explore the excitement of Los Angeles. Rosa and I loved to dance. I must say that I know how to shake my hips! Nick often reminds me about the time I danced onstage with Sting at a Breast Cancer Research Foundation benefit dinner at the Waldorf Astoria in New York. Rosa and I explored the LA club scene. We would drive to LA after work during the week to dance to house, hip-hop, and '90s pop at the American clubs and then to Latin hip-hop and pop at the Latin clubs in LA and Orange County on weekends.

On one of our nights out, we met two Latino guys at the local Latin club, J.C. Fandango. The two were best friends and both were business owners. I was instantly attracted to Pepito, a Cubano three years older than me. He was attractive but not drop-dead gorgeous. But he swept me off my feet with his big personality and wicked sense of humor. We were friends before a romantic relationship developed. The four of us hung out together and enjoyed each other's company.

Pepito owned a bakery. One day he invited me over to learn how to bake bread. Watching him at work revealed a side of Pepito that wasn't readily apparent. There he was dressed in old jeans and a torn T-shirt, with dough up to his elbows, guiding me as I attempted to make my first loaf of bread.

"The secret is in how much you knead it," he said as he smiled at me.

I was hooked! Pepito may have dressed like a bum at work, but outside of the bakery he liked to dress up; Armani suits were his signature look. He loved to party and to eat out, and for the first time in my life I let myself be spoiled by someone else. I had had only one boyfriend up until then, but my relationship with Pablo had been very different: we were both students, I was living at home, and we could not afford to do more than simple things. Pepito and I made an attractive couple, pulling up to restaurants in his Lexus ES 300 and being escorted to the roped-off VIP areas in clubs.

I never wanted to be owned by anyone, especially a man. I wanted to forge my own way in life on my own terms, but with Pepito I felt protected, and it felt nice! He whisked me off for a romantic weekend skiing in Tahoe, and we partied in Vegas with his friends. I had never lived like this before, and it felt nice to be cared for in a relationship. I caught myself at times wondering whether this was it: *Was he the one?*

We never discussed marriage; however, his mom and sister—whom I adored—did. I always deflected, telling them it was too early for me to get married. I didn't know how to explain to them that I was hearing an inner voice telling me that maybe Pepito wasn't the one, that there was still so much more to do.

I had gone from midnight curfews in Puerto Rico to being in the Hollywood social scene and enjoying glamorous weekends. For the first time in my life I was experiencing life and love freely without rules or guidelines, without anyone looking over my shoulder: no neighbors to tattle, no parents watching. I was discovering myself in new and exciting ways.

But just as soon as I had really begun to enjoy this new exciting world, everything came crashing down.

I persuaded Pepito to take a trip to Puerto Rico to meet Mami, my friends, and the rest of my family. This was the first time I had been back to Puerto Rico. It was a very emotional visit. Mami was overjoyed to see me and I felt my own tears welling up as I hugged her. Everyone loved Pepito, and several of my girlfriends asked, "Is he the one?"

I wasn't sure how to answer, and even if I had been tied to a polygraph machine and asked to tell the truth, I don't know what I would have said. The ten days I spent in Puerto Rico were moving but also revealing. If I had any doubts about my decision to leave, they were dispelled during those ten days. Hanging out with my childhood friends was incredible; we shared stories, laughed, and cried. But I saw how their lives were just as they had been when I was there before: nothing had changed. But *I* had changed: my life was now very different, and I was experiencing many of the things I hoped to experience. As I said goodbye to Mami, she could sense the change in me, too, and didn't make even the slightest attempt to persuade me to stay.

After we returned to LA, Pepito needed to get back to the bakery and asked me to drop him off and drive to my apartment in Costa Mesa. He told me he would pick up the car later.

On my way to Costa Mesa, a cat ran into the middle of the road. Instinctively, I slammed on the brakes. The car came to an abrupt stop and a bunch of things on the back seat came tumbling forward. When I got to the apartment, I picked up the items that had fallen onto the floor. As I picked up Pepito's black organizer, I realized the zipper had not been closed and all the contents had spilled out. I came across a Polaroid photo. There were four people in the photo, Pepito and one of his best friends from LA and two girls I didn't recognize. As I looked more closely, I could see Pepito with his arm around one of the two girls. I could not help myself: I searched through the other papers and pulled out an LA hotel bill and restaurant receipt, dated a month earlier. Pepito had spent that weekend in LA, telling me he was staying at his friend's apartment, that they needed to catch up and his friend had some issues he needed to discuss. Why, then, was there a hotel bill for two guests and a restaurant bill for four? And then I knew: Pepito had cheated on me.

When I confronted Pepito later that evening, he admitted he had cheated and said it meant nothing. It was just a one-night fling. One night or one weekend—it didn't matter to me. Our relationship ended that evening. My heart was broken—again. I couldn't reconcile that not twenty-four hours earlier, Pepito had been talking and laughing with my family, knowing he had cheated on me. I had had two long-term relationships, both with Latino men, and both had ended when they were unfaithful. Maybe Latino men were not for me. I wanted to find a love that was exciting and intoxicating but at the same time strong and stable. I then knew it would probably take me some time to find what I was looking for.

My two relationships had given me lessons in love. I would keep searching. I know that from that moment through every relationship I've had since, I have learned a bit more of what it is I am truly looking for in a partner.

For the next month I returned to my old routine: working at the stores during the week and, instead of going out and partying, staying at home to read and contemplate. It was 1996, and the second anniversary of my arrival in California was approaching. It had been a roller-coaster ride, I had grown in so many ways, but for the first time I had a flicker of self-doubt. Was I really on the right path? Working in stores was not my long-term plan. There was more to do than just party every night. I needed to decide on a career and find a job that would allow me to go back and finish college. But as I mulled this over, another temporary distraction befell me.

When I broke up with Pepito, Rosa was very understanding and a good listener. However, after four weeks of "mourning," as she put it, it was time to get out, so Rosa and her friends took me to a famous celebrity-filled club on La Cienega

Boulevard called the Gate. It was one of those places where people got selected to go inside. This was a different world yet again. My evening at the Gate was just what I needed: the old adage about getting back on the horse after you are thrown was certainly true. Our visits to the Gate became regular weekend occurrences. We became friends with the club promoters and were invited to the VIP areas, where we partied and even had cocktails with Madonna on one occasion and met and danced with Luis Miguel, who was performing in Los Angeles as part of his El Concierto tour.

I am a music lover and love many Latin artists, most of whom stopped off in LA during their tours. Maná was one of the favorite soft-rock bands I listened to during my teens and at college. When we heard they were playing in Los Angeles, Rosa and I had to get tickets. As soon as the tickets went on sale, we called up the box office and scored front-row seats to their concert. Dressed to the nines and ready to sing our hearts out, we impatiently waited for the concert to start. Just before the lights dimmed, a gentleman came up to us, remarked that we were clearly Maná fans, and asked whether we would like to go backstage and meet the band after the performance. The man turned out to be the band's manager and promoter. We accepted—*of course*! Not only did we party with them that night, but they invited us to meet them at all the other concerts during the West Coast leg of their tour. Eventually we were on a first-name basis with the members of the group and hanging out with them after their concerts. This was yet again a whole new experience for me, a world I hadn't seen before. I had heard about groupies and what went on in the hotel suites after concerts with rock stars, but Maná were perfect gentlemen.

One Sunday we got a call from the promoter to say he was also managing the Enrique Iglesias tour. Then he asked if we wanted to attend the San Diego show. Of course! We got to meet Enrique backstage and then two weeks later were invited to San Jose for another of his concerts. It was a heady world, and exhausting, but I needed to get back to finding my life path.

What I needed was a permanent position in a company with growth opportunities. Searching the wanted ads, I stumbled across a temp job in the automotive industry, working in the legal department for a major car manufacturer. I had not planned to work in the automotive industry or in a legal department, but I needed a start. Little did I know that this temp position would be the gateway to my life as a career woman.

I began in November 1996 as a temp. After eight months the company offered me a permanent position. Yippee—I now had health benefits, which took a big worry off my shoulders. I had a pension plan. This was my first proper job.

For the first year I put my head down, worked hard, and enjoyed the security of a full-time job. I had many expectations about what I hoped to achieve. The one thing I did not think I would find was love!

I was working on one of the many legal cases that I managed for the finance arm of the company but had reached a roadblock with one particular case. A woman had defaulted on her car loan payments and had disappeared along with her car. After exhausting all efforts, Juliana, my boss, suggested I take it to senior executive Jonathan Stone for his assistance. His team looked after the warranty and service operation and could maybe provide information on the car and therefore the woman's whereabouts. I was apprehensive about contacting Jonathan, but nonetheless his executive assistant put me on his calendar for a face-to-face meeting that same week.

When I walked into Jonathan's office, my inner voice whispered, *You are gonna date him!* I pushed the voice to the back of my mind. I was there to sort out a pressing legal case. But when he stood up from behind his desk, I found myself standing in front of a six-foot silver fox. He held out his hand and smiled. I melted inside.

I presented the case to him. I am normally a confident person, but I stumbled over my words, occasionally looking up from my papers into his deep-blue eyes, feeling myself beginning to flush. What was going on?

Was it his demeanor? His presence that filled the room? Or the confidence and poise he exuded? The more we spoke, the more I sensed he felt the same curiosity about me. I knew our exchange at that point was meant to be strictly professional. I thanked him for his help and left his office, not expecting to see him again.

He came by my cubicle the next day to tell me something about my case he had overlooked during our meeting. Over the next two weeks he worked with me to solve the case; we were like Mulder and Scully tracking down leads while trying to ignore the chemistry that was building between us. During one conversation about the case he said, "If we are able to recover this car, we should celebrate; lunch will be on me."

I didn't know what to think. He was a highly successful executive at the company, twenty-five years my senior. This was highly irregular, unexpected, and not a situation I knew how to handle. A couple of weeks later we finally solved the case and, true to his word, Jonathan invited me to a celebratory lunch. Not sure whether to accept, I went straight to Juliana for her advice. She certainly raised an eyebrow when I told her about the invitation but smiled and said to enjoy the lunch.

Jonathan and I couldn't have come from more opposite worlds. I was a young Latina woman in my twenties, starting out my career, while Jonathan was a highly successful man who was recently divorced after a twenty-year marriage. He had two teenage boys.

But when we sat down at the table that day for lunch, my nerves were replaced by the undeniable chemistry that pulled us closer. The sparks that started flying that day ignited what would become a deep and meaningful relationship that continued off and on for six years. Once we officially started dating, we followed company protocol by informing our bosses of the relationship—in my case Juliana and in his case the CEO of the company.

Jonathan was whip smart and enjoyed sharing with me his wealth of knowledge and the experiences he had accumulated during a highly successful automotive industry career. He taught me about how a dealership operates and who the best vendors were and let me sit in on meetings with the heads of other automotive companies. During the time we spent together, *Automotive News* named him one of the top executives in the automotive industry, an honor that filled me with pride. I observed his leadership skills carefully and soaked up how he handled difficult work situations while managing to be a mentor to his team. While I was a sponge that absorbed every drop of information and advice he had to professionally offer, I also felt us become partners in mind and spirit and was also able to give back and help him. Although incredibly adept in the office and a skilled manager of people, his relationship with his children was a struggle, exacerbated by his divorce. I helped him bridge that gap, and in the process I became very close to both his sons. Jonathan encouraged me to complete my degree and helped me enroll in night classes to obtain an accelerated business degree. With Jonathan as my mentor, my newly resumed studies, and the experiences I was getting, I knew not only that I belonged in corporate America, but that I would excel. It was the first time I realized I could be a senior executive.

But beyond the office, we enjoyed life to the fullest. Before I met Jonathan, I had never left the United States. My dream had always been to travel, to visit the wonderful capitals of Europe and soak up the cultures I had only read about in magazines and seen on TV. And in the fall of 1998, eighteen months after we started dating, I traveled to Europe with Jonathan to Milan, London, and Paris—places my inner voice had always told me I'd go.

Eventually our relationship came to a standstill. Jonathan's role meant he traveled often to Asia, all over the United States, and Europe. When he came back from trips, he only wanted to stay home and not go anywhere. Although his cup overflowed with the qualities that I desired in a partner, our life together became monotonous and—dare I say it?—dull. Jonathan was an introvert, preferred to stay in, and was very much set in his ways; I, on the other hand, was very much the extrovert and yearned for a partner with a sense of adventure. I also realized that a twenty-five-year age difference would become a bigger issue for me down the road.

Jonathan had already traveled, made mistakes, become successful, and fulfilled his dream of having children, while I was still a work in progress. At the time, I envisioned marriage and children, and Jonathan wanted nothing of the sort. He wasn't interested in doing it all over again at that point in his life, although at first, during the beginning of our relationship, he was open to it. I thought that I could change his mind, but I couldn't. Although I loved and admired Jonathan, it became the ultimate deal breaker that would result in the slow and steady demise of our relationship.

Ending my relationship with Jonathan was extremely difficult. I couldn't make a clean break like I had with Pablo or Pepito. Jonathan had not cheated on me or done anything to hurt me. I had simply learned that our relationship was in the present. Talking about the future made him uncomfortable, uneasy, whereas I had a whole life ahead of me. I realized that the most important thing was to find someone you can build a future with, not just a present. Even though my inner voice told me it was the right thing, I was extremely scared to let go of him completely and went back to him on four or five occasions. But eventually we both knew the relationship had run its course. We finally parted in the fall of 2003, and although I think of Jonathan with fondness, we have never met since.

Building and visualizing the future is what my entire life has been about, even when that future is hanging from a thread.

5

A Midlife Hurricane

Be thou the rainbow in the storms of life!
The evening beam that smiles the clouds away,
and tints to-morrow with prophetic ray!
—LORD BYRON

By the start of the new millennium, I had hit my stride. My twenties were coming to a close, with many important yet difficult lessons in love behind me. A traumatic event at work, followed by an unexpected opportunity, had launched a career in the world of Hispanic advertising and marketing. I was doing something I was passionate about. I was traveling the world, making new friends, and embracing every opportunity I encountered. Little did I know I was in the eye of a storm. But I am getting ahead of myself.

I sailed through the start of my twenties with a generally clean bill of health. But the latter part of the '90s provided an unwelcome preview of what was to unfold over the next ten years. It was 1999, I had just turned twenty-six, and suddenly, out of the blue, my body started acting up. I had bouts of intense pain in my pelvic area. These were not run-of-the-mill period cramps; they were at another level. When I mentioned this issue to my gynecologist at my annual checkup, she suspected

I might have endometriosis, so she decided to perform an exploratory laparoscopy to get to the bottom of my discomfort.

The surgery revealed that her suspicions were wrong. Instead she discovered fibroids, which are noncancerous tumors in the uterus that usually appear during a woman's childbearing years. While there was nothing to do about this other than keep a close eye on my body, she did break some unexpected news to me: she had discovered that my uterus itself was deformed, which meant that carrying a child to term might be difficult.

I was speechless. At the time, the idea of having children was still on my radar—so much so that it had been one of the deal breakers in my relationship with Jonathan and would be the deal breaker in relationships yet to come with men who were not interested in going down that road. Back then I felt that having children was a part of my womanhood, a must, so learning that it wouldn't be easy to carry my own child was devastating to say the least. I also couldn't imagine telling a guy I liked that I couldn't have kids because my uterus was deformed! My heart sank, naturally, as I tried to wrap my mind around the reality of the news. I decided that if there came a moment when having children became a priority in my life, I would figure out a way to make it happen. That was that.

This news came at a terrible time in my life. It all began with a change in the management structure at work. In a matter of days, life as I knew it at work went from motivating and stimulating—a place where I looked forward to going every morning—to an absolute living hell.

My new boss was a senior executive of the company, and as soon as I started reporting to him, he began to sexually harass me. He was a grotesque, out-of-shape man who thought his position and power gave him the right to abuse me and demand sexual favors. I had encountered sexual harassment once before, back on the University of Puerto Rico's Mayagüez campus, when a professor came on to me in a clear and unwelcome way with sexual gestures and innuendo, a total violation of the university's rules of conduct. I swatted him away each time and after the third advance he backed away. However, my situation at work was an altogether different situation. I never knew the lengths a man would go to try to get his way. And when he didn't get it, the punishment he would mete out was horrific.

I thought that after a few stern rebuffs the man would get the message and the harassment would stop. But each time I rejected his advances, the situation became worse. He would come on to me with renewed vigor.

I decided to formally report him, filing two formal written complaints to the head of the human resources department. Nothing was done in response to my complaints. The abuse continued. I was desperate. His pursuit had become a sick kind of power play: he needed to have me because he was my superior, and I wouldn't let him.

My life became a living nightmare. I cried myself to sleep, afraid of waking up and going to work. I asked myself continuously, *Why doesn't HR do something to help me?* But deep down inside I knew why. I was a twenty-six-year-old Latina, and he was an important executive. It was his word against mine. They decided to ignore me and pretend the problem didn't exist or that it would go away. His intimidation tactics moved out into the open. He would appear at my cubicle, place his hands on the frame, put his face as close to mine as he could, and then whisper that if I didn't sleep with him, he would double my workload or fire me. And sure enough, every time I said no, he made sure I paid the price. The more I turned him down, the more work he piled on my desk with impossible deadlines.

After my first two formal complaints, I continued to document every incident and deliver letters to human resources describing every incident and occasion, but it was like being locked in a room in the middle of nowhere, screaming at the top of my lungs while no one heard me and no one cared. Human resources eventually sent me a letter stating they would talk to him. I knew I would pay for that.

Sure enough, his interest in me became an obsession. He started to follow me everywhere, like an unwanted shadow. On one occasion he followed me in his car all the way home. I felt terrified, helpless, alone. A thousand times I thought about quitting my job and moving far away, but every time I came to the same conclusion: Why did I have to change my entire life when I had done nothing wrong? Why did I have to walk away from a job I loved because someone else was behaving improperly? It didn't seem fair, and besides, I think I was so worn down at that point that I don't think I would have been capable of making such a bold move.

Everything about me began to change. My demeanor changed; I became somber and reserved; I changed the way I dressed. I have always been a fashionable woman who put a great deal of effort into looking good—just like Mami taught me—but it got to a point where I no longer found any pleasure in making myself look good in the morning and certainly didn't want to attract any admiring advances from my boss. I doubted myself a great deal, and although I was attractive, I found myself purposely wanting to look ugly. I didn't want to call any attention to myself, so I exchanged my fitted button-down shirts for loose turtlenecks and loose suits, stopped putting on makeup, severely pulled my hair back every day, and kept to myself as much as possible in the hope that my boss would stop his advances.

Six months went by, during which I dreaded the morning alarm clock as if it were my daily death sentence. It was like living in my own nightmarish Groundhog Day, until one day the monster called me into his office and gave me an ultimatum.

"I just want you to know that it doesn't matter how many times you report me, you are stuck with me. You have no choice. You have to deal with me whether you like it or not."

Trembling from head to toe out of fear, disgust, and rage, I stormed out of his office, slammed the door behind me, and marched straight to the human resources department. However, as soon as I tried to articulate the most recent incident, my body shut down and I belly flopped into a full-blown nervous breakdown, hysterically crying, my body shaking uncontrollably. It was such a forceful physical reaction to months of aggressive harassment, the head of human resources had to call an ambulance as I gasped for air. I was rushed to the hospital for medical assistance. It was clear: There was no going back. The aggression had been so prolonged and violent that by the time I had my nervous breakdown, I could barely recognize my strong-minded, determined self. I was a shell of the woman I once was, and it was only now, looking back, that I realize how far I had fallen.

I needed professional help. I found a great therapist, went to weekly sessions, started Bikram Yoga, and I was referred to a psychiatrist who prescribed antidepressants. The thought of being on antidepressant medication made me sick to my stomach. I took them for only three months, because I was scared of dependency, and decided to pursue alternative relaxation methods like yoga and meditation. I was formally diagnosed with post-traumatic stress disorder (PTSD). Until then I thought that term only applied to war veterans. Little did I know how PTSD would color my life.

I decided to hire an attorney to help me deal with the company, which, after much back and forth, ultimately said that they would settle out of court. But the best news was that the monster had been fired. I later found out that once I left the company after the nervous breakdown, he started to harass an assistant in his department and she hired Gloria Allred as her lawyer. I know this because Gloria's office called me to see if I would be willing to testify about how he had harassed me. I did, and my testimony helped her case. She got a six-figure payout. All I really wanted was my job back. And I got that along with some money. I agreed not to disclose the amount, so I will only say that I didn't make enough money to retire on!

Now, in the era of #MeToo and #TimesUp, when so many women have come forward to share their horrific stories of sexual harassment and assault, it's hard to understand how we have all—and I mean both men and women—allowed such levels of abuse to happen under our noses. I am so glad it has been exposed, but I have also found myself reliving that terrible period in my life. The scar is for a lifetime. I hope that in the future no woman ever has to endure what I had to endure—not from a boss, not from a spouse, not from an acquaintance or a colleague—and that younger generations of women, including my beloved nine-year-old niece, have to only read about this in the history books as a thing of the past.

After a three-month absence, I returned to work. I switched

from the financial arm of the company to the manufacturer marketing-advertising department as the Hispanic marketing senior specialist. It was a big job. I suspected they offered me the role partly because I was the only Spanish speaker in the company, and, gosh, did I have to work hard to prove myself in this new role. By now most people in the office saw me as the girl who had been harassed, but my new boss saw me as the girl who had been harassed, sued the company, and now needed to be taught advertising and marketing!

I had to fight, over and over again, not to allow him to treat me like an assistant. I wanted to be treated with the respect the role deserved. Yet every time I met a new face from an ad agency or the media they would tell me, "Oh, he told us you are the new assistant"—and I would cringe and have to correct them. Then later I would confront my boss and let him know I wasn't his assistant; I was the Hispanic marketing senior specialist. It took a lot of time and many disagreements with him, but slowly he warmed to me. I showed him I was a hard worker. I wouldn't leave work if he was still in the office and always made sure to do more than I was asked. He was naïve to judge me, but once he finally gave me a real chance and his support, it paid off. I led the office's Hispanic marketing efforts, learned the industry, and increased Hispanic sales by 300 percent in my three years in the job. My boss and I became good friends and are still friends to this day.

By the time I turned thirty years old, I had landed my first six-figure job. The Bravo Group was at that time the number one Hispanic ad agency in the country and part of the renowned global ad agency Young & Rubicam. I followed Bravo closely and working for them was my dream, a goal that seemed out of reach. But in April 2002 I got my first-ever call from a headhunter looking to recruit an account director for The Bravo Group! I listened to what the headhunter had to say, agreed to meet with Bravo, and without hesitation accepted their offer to move from the client side of the marketing world to the agency side. I had finally found my calling. I loved my career on the agency side. I loved the work. I loved the people. I loved working with the media. I was nominated by the CEO of The Bravo Group to a global Young & Rubicam senior leadership program designed by McKinsey & Company to train and develop the leaders of the future. I was one of twenty selected from nominees from all over the world. One of my most memorable professional experiences was attending the weeklong program held in Bangkok, Thailand, with other global senior executives.

My new income also allowed me to buy my first home in California: a two-story condo on the hill overlooking the mountains in Trabuco Canyon. I lovingly furnished each room with help from my good friend Monica, an interior designer. We chose the wallpaper, window treatments, furniture, and art. I had arrived! I was living the American dream my *tío* Rafael had talked to me about. But just as everything finally began to fall into place, my health took yet another beating.

It started with abdominal discomfort. I would feel a sudden cramp, and then an intense need to rush to the nearest restroom, lock the door, and sit on the toilet, but to no avail. My body was crying out that a bowel movement was forthcoming. But then . . . nothing. *Nada*. That was when anxiety mixed with the anticipation kicked in and triggered panic attacks. My heart would start to race, sweat would pour down my face, and my hair would be drenched within minutes as if I had been running on a treadmill for an hour.

The gastroenterologist could not put his finger on the cause of this type of constipation. I tried different specialists without finding the reason and an entire year went by with me experiencing frequent bouts of panic attacks until I was finally referred to a special gastrointestinal medical research team at UCLA Medical Center. I was told I had a severe form of irritable bowel syndrome (IBS). Although the exact cause of IBS is not known, doctors think it may result from a disturbance in the way the gut, brain, and nervous system interact. The team concluded that my IBS was probably triggered by the PTSD stemming from my sexual harassment. Here I was, three years after closing out the sexual harassment matter, but my body had suffered long-term consequences.

I have come to learn that everything we feel and experience has some sort of physical and mental consequence, even if we don't actually sense or see it at the time—something I would continue to explore on a deeper level over the years as my health continued to surprise me.

At the time, we didn't know as much about IBS as we do now, and there were no treatments or drugs, so the only thing I could do to relieve my symptoms was to change my diet and avoid unnecessary stress—easier said than done in this modern world of ours. Once again I did my best to follow the doctor's orders; however, every time I felt the need to go to the bathroom, the anxiety was so out of control that I would break into a full panic attack. The toilet became my mortal enemy, and a place that I now associated with sweats, galloping heartbeats, and outright fear of the pain that would ensue as I tried to convince my body to do what every other normal human being does on a daily basis without even batting an eyelid. It had a crippling effect on my body. I tried to learn how to cope with the panic attacks. Sometimes my team at The Bravo Group would comment about me coming in to work after 9:00 a.m., when everyone else had been at their desks for over an hour. But what they didn't know was the time I would spend at home dealing with wild panic attacks during a morning bowel movement. They had no idea what I was going through and why.

Despite the IBS, I grew my accounts exponentially and I was eventually green-lighted to hire a larger team. As I built the team up, I traveled to New York and Miami every month to oversee their work on my clients' accounts and develop business relationships with new clients. I was on a professional high, mingling with top-notch marketing and advertising executives, meeting media moguls, attending red-carpet events, and rubbing shoulders with celebs as I made a name for myself in this competitive but exhilarating field. In May 2003 the TV network "upfronts"—the television industry's all-important gathering among network executives, advertisers, and the press—found me in my beloved New York City meeting with colleagues and clients, ready to talk business and network like a champion for the entire week.

I went to lunch with two television network associates and one of them offered me a sip of his cocktail; against my better judgment, I took it. A couple of hours later he went on to tell me ever so casually that he was recovering from mononucleosis! I could not believe it: I did not need mono on top of everything else! Throughout the rest of the evening I kept mentally checking myself over to see if I had any symptoms. I collapsed into bed exhausted but feeling fine. The next day I awoke to flu-like symptoms and a fever of 103. The hotel doctor prescribed some antibiotics, told me to rest and relax. But two days later I still wasn't feeling any better. It felt like my body was shutting down. The fever remained and I couldn't even get up to go to the bathroom. This time the doctor sent an ambulance for me and I was admitted to the hospital. When the lab results came back, not surprisingly, they indicated infectious mononucleosis. My white blood cell count had tanked and I was forced to stay in the hospital for the next ten days.

Under any other circumstances, I probably wouldn't have minded spending some restful time in a bed, but staying ten days in the hospital meant I would miss my sister Jessica's bachelorette party, which I had been planning for her. While my family gathered in California to help my sister prepare for one of the happiest days of her life, I was stuck in a hospital bed 3,500 miles away.

Jessica had moved to California a couple of years after I left Puerto Rico. When I saw everything California had to offer, I urged her to come check it out for herself. I knew she could do so much more with her life if she, too, took that leap of faith. She fell in love with California, got a job, and never moved back to Puerto Rico. That decision eventually led her to meet her future husband, Rocco. Originally from Jordan, Rocco is a beach boy at heart, happiest in flip-flops and shorts, and is the most awesome brother-in-law in the world. Later they would have the two most treasured children in my life, who are just filled with light: my smarty-pants nephew, Jam Jam, was born in 2005, and my princess niece, Marie, who loves unicorns, rainbows, and anything that sparkles as much as I do, was born in 2009. Jam Jam and Marie are undoubtedly the two kids I never had.

Suffice to say that while I lay in that hospital bed in New York, doing my best to recover from mono, I felt a mixture of boredom and unimaginable frustration. Dr. Stein, the doctor who had attended to me in the hotel, kept me sane and looked after me until I was released and able to fly home to California to make it in time for my sister's wedding day. Despite the fact I was still running a fever of 102 and popping Tylenol pills every four hours, I had a great time. Many of my childhood friends had flown in from Puerto Rico for Jessica's wedding, and for the first time in my adult life Mami and her entire side of the family were reunited. It was a very joyous occasion.

Dr. Stein had advised me to follow up with my gastroenterologist once I got back home. As it turned out, whether it was from the mono or the effects of my IBS, I was now suffering from a rectal prolapse that, sadly, would require yet another surgery. But this time I would have the best nurse in the world by my side, as Mami had postponed her return to Puerto Rico to care for me.

I really struggled with the aftereffects of the rectal surgery, especially the intense pain. It felt as if someone were slowly tearing away at my colon with a paper shredder. The day I was released from the hospital, I ended up having to go back to the ER because the pain medicine just wasn't strong enough.

The ER resident decided to do a rectal exam, which caused me to scream out at the top of my lungs, tears rolling down my cheeks. I am sure the entire ER area and even people in the parking lot heard my screams. A team of doctors arrived within seconds by my bedside and I was hospitalized for another week just for pain management. I remember I had a morphine pump that I would push anytime I wanted. I was asleep more than I was awake; in fact, I was asleep more than I had ever been during any other one-week period of my life. It was an awful feeling being sedated to that degree 24/7. What no one had the decency to tell me was that morphine causes constipation. Duh! I felt like I was on a roller coaster without being able to get off. I regretted ever sipping from that stranger's cocktail. I heard a little voice telling me over and over: *Remember, your mom has always said never to drink from any person's glass.* I had brought this on myself. No one else was to blame. I felt the stress of being away from work. I worried I would get fired, although I was on medical leave. I felt powerless. But there was one final kicker: once released from the hospital, I went through morphine withdrawal, a nasty experience that scared me to death. I kept telling myself that I would never take a painkiller again. Between not being able to sit down for any length of time and the morphine withdrawal, it took me an entire month to recover!

Once I had healed, I decided to treat myself to an afternoon at the spa at the Montage Laguna Beach, one of my favorite spots on earth, to relax and to pamper myself after what I had been through. Little did I know that the angels I have always felt watch over me would secretly plot to make a silly little dream of mine come true. During all those weeks in the New York hospital and while recovering at home in California, I never missed an episode of Ellen DeGeneres's talk show. I became obsessed with her and the program. I laughed. I cried. I laughed more than I cried. I mean, she's hilarious. I had already put out into the universe that I wanted to meet her someday or attend her show through my media connections.

Well, wouldn't you know that, once I finished having my massage that day at the spa, I took off my clothes—yep, fully naked—and jumped into the Jacuzzi. I was minding my own business, listening to the waterfall, taking long, deep breaths. I was all alone with not another soul in sight, when suddenly

I heard footsteps. I didn't even bother to look up, but I did catch the sight of a person's feet at the top of the steps entering the Jacuzzi, then her body, as fully naked as I was, before she sat down in the Jacuzzi in front of me. After some time I decided to look up at the face of my fellow nude bather and couldn't believe my eyes. It was Ellen!

"Oh my God, it's you!" I said.

"Yep, it's me," she laughed.

I told her that I had been watching her show every day for the past few months while recovering from an illness, and after joking that most people who watched her show were sick, Ellen said that she was really sorry to hear that I had been ill and hoped I was okay now. Minutes later, her girlfriend Portia de Rossi climbed in. I wanted to scream! She said hello, and Ellen asked my name so she could introduce me, and when I said it was "Zulema," she said, "I think it's better if I call you Zebra."

The episode validated one of my core beliefs: What you put out to the universe, the universe gives back to you.

After my extended absence from work, I needed to get back to my teams and my clients. For the next three months I put in the hours and made sure that I was on top of everything that was going on. I was still commuting back and forth between California and New York, but now I was traveling to Miami and South America to shoot commercials for my clients. My biggest client was Mazda, and although they were an established presence in the United States, their brand awareness and market share in the Hispanic sector was limited. My job: to build a marketing campaign and put the company on the map. I rarely saw my new apartment in Orange County during this period of my life and got to know the real meaning of "living out of a suitcase." I have always been conscientious about fulfilling the commitments I make, but I know I put in the extra effort to show that I still "had it" after my medical absence—that I was still able to compete with the best and deep down knew that I had to put in the extra effort because I was a woman in a male-dominated automotive world. I didn't want to give anyone a reason to question my ability to do my job. The hours were grueling, but I got the result I wanted: a well-received TV campaign and greater-than-expected ratings that increased Mazda's Hispanic market share by 10 percent quarter over quarter. I felt a mixture of elation and relief: I had shown I was still a force to be reckoned with.

There was a side benefit to all this. I got to meet a group of media executives from Chicago, Miami, and New York who later became my travel partners in crime. They all worked for the same TV network and I was their client who became their friend. In our personal lives, we were all at the same place, at the right time. We were single, we shared a love for travel and good living, and we all worked and traveled like maniacs. The saying "Work hard, play hard" completely fitted us. We began to plan, coordinate our schedules, and take full advantage of any long weekend afforded us to meet at different destinations throughout the world. This idea began while two of us were reading the newspaper travel section while sunbathing in Miami. We got excited about spending a weekend at Punta Cana in the Dominican Republic. No sooner had we suggested it to the group than our flights were booked for the following weekend. A weekend in Chicago followed. Then Miami and New York. We each took turns planning a trip and somehow every trip managed to top the one before it. Over Thanksgiving weekend in 2004, we traveled to Argentina and Brazil. That was my trip to plan, as I had been to Argentina many times. While sipping caipirinhas on Ipanema Beach, I came up with the next crazy adventure: to run a marathon! But of course, this wasn't going to be just any marathon but one we could all get entries into. After a little research and a few phone calls, we had it: Rome in March! I began training right then and there, on the gorgeous Ipanema Beach.

When I got home, I continued running every day so that I would do my best on race day. Since I was a rookie, I decided to run the marathon with Team in Training, a nonprofit that funds lymphoma research. I needed guidance and also wanted to run for a purpose. Rosa's mom had recently passed away from brain cancer, and Juliana—the best boss I ever had from the car company—had been recently diagnosed with lymphoma, so picking Team in Training was a natural choice for me. When I finally got to the starting line in Rome, I had raised over $6,000 for lymphoma research and treatment—a harbinger of my future purpose, although I was unaware of this back then.

I flew to Chicago on weekends to train with fellow Team in Training runners. I picked Chicago, because that was where two from the group who were going to run the marathon with me lived. As the date grew nearer, a local half marathon in Huntington Beach, California, was my checkpoint on how my training was going. I finished in a little over two hours. I was ready!

When I landed in Rome in March 2005, there was palpable excitement in the air that blended with my own nervousness. I had already been to Rome with Jonathan, but this trip was very different. It marked my independence. As I ran past the Piazza Navona and the Spanish Steps, alongside the walls of

Vatican City, and past the Trevi Fountain, it seemed more like a private sightseeing tour. I was taking it all in and constantly acknowledging that this would be the experience of a lifetime. Finishing my first marathon was a badge of honor, like a college degree that nobody can take away from you. I now belonged to a special club—those who, against all odds, put their bodies through pain and suffering to run 26.2 miles—and for me it was in the name of doing good.

When I returned home to Orange County, I had two days to relax before flying back to New York for business meetings. As the meetings progressed, my marathon fatigue and jet lag did not subside, and it was accompanied by a butterfly rash on my face.

At first I didn't think too much of this, but it persisted. Since I was in New York City, I went to see Dr. Stein. After evaluating my symptoms and running blood work, I was diagnosed with lupus. I didn't know anything about lupus except that one of my mom's friends had died from the disease in her late twenties. It was the first autoimmune disorder I had encountered in my life. However, within three months, my antinuclear antibody (ANA) levels had normalized, leading the doctor to conclude that what I had actually suffered was "temporary lupus." I don't even know if this is really a condition. I attributed my symptoms to the strain I put my body through during the marathon. Without any reason to question the doctor, I carried on. No lupus? Okay. Check!

I now wonder if that doctor made a mistake by not following up on this. I will never really know, but given the slew of ailments that rained on my body's parade during the following decade, including a proper lupus diagnosis, it's hard not to think that this may have been the case. Perhaps I was showing an early stage of the disease, which deserved to be monitored, versus a temporary diagnosis.

⎰⎱

After almost four years at The Bravo Group, I had progressed from being an account director to being a group managing director. I now managed a team of twelve and had grown the client base, bringing on Land Rover and Jaguar as two major new clients. I was in Thailand for the Leaders of the Future training program and I knew that, despite all the drama experienced, the illness setbacks endured, I was finally comfortable in my own skin. I was the butterfly that had emerged from the cocoon and spread her wings. Yet getting the balance right between my professional and family lives has always been something I've struggled with. As I was boarding the plane in Bangkok to fly home at the end of the training program, I got the phone call on my BlackBerry from Mami to tell me that I was now an auntie. Jessica had given birth to Jam Jam earlier than expected. I had desperately wanted to be there for his birth, but he was healthy; that was all that mattered. I sat on the plane, willing it to go faster with every minute. When the plane touched down, I seriously considered leaving my luggage on the baggage claim to speed up my exit from the airport! Being a *titi* is the best feeling in the world. Holding Jam Jam for the first time was like holding my own newborn child.

⎰⎱

My time back home with my Jam Jam gave me time to reflect on where I was both personally and professionally. My love life was definitely still a work in progress, and if I had to grade myself, I would probably have to give a "below expectations" assessment.

Professionally, I realized I was ready for the next challenge, and I didn't have to wait long before it arrived: a job in Manhattan with a competitor, working for Jeff, my first boss at Bravo. I jumped at the chance. My interest in art, food, and fashion made me crave the Big Apple. Europe was just across the pond, home to the cities, architecture, and culture I was most drawn to. My dating scene also needed a change. I wasn't tall and blond with big breasts and stick-thin like women in Orange County—the type that men in Southern California seemed to go for—and I wanted a man with a stamped passport.

I formally accepted the offer and agreed to start in October 2006. One of the negotiating points of my offer was my insistence that the company transport my modest wine collection to New York. During my trips to Argentina, I had acquired a nice collection of Malbecs, carefully stored in a small wine fridge in my apartment. I had grown to learn quite a lot about wine over the previous four years. Several of the dealers I interacted with had extensive wine collections, and most of the TV network heads I knew and had dinner with loved wine. Little did I know how important wine appreciation and collecting would become in my future.

So I rented out my apartment in California and set out on my New York adventure living in a 1,000-square-foot corporate apartment with a terrace overlooking Madison Square Park, in front of one of my favorite restaurants: Eleven Madison Park. I was "living the dream" as a single woman.

I thought I had it all. With unobstructed views east and west, I could watch the sun rise and set in my new home; I was the number two in command of the New York office, set to run a $90 million advertising budget, and I had met a gorgeous Dolce & Gabbana and Calvin Klein underwear model. My new beau made me feel like Samantha Jones from *Sex and the City*. I'll never forget driving through the Lincoln Tunnel from Newark Airport and seeing him on one of those massive billboards. This was my New York City life!

However, the reality of the job quickly set in. I was soon working incredibly long hours day in and day out, clients were extremely demanding, and I was overworked. I suddenly went from "having it all" to having no life to speak of. My dream of *living* in New York turned into the reality of returning to my apartment to simply sleep. I no longer had free time to enjoy the city. The next twelve months were a blur as one week merged into the next. I didn't even get to travel home to see my family. After Jam Jam was born, Mami decided to stay in California and live with my sister to help look after her grandson. I was so busy, I didn't even get to see her, my sister, my brother-in-law, or Jam Jam.

My life has always been a series of whirlwinds, each one starting out innocuously, spinning slowly, then accelerating and pulling in everything around, reaching its crescendo as it rattles windows and shakes foundations before dying out. My New York whirlwind was gearing up for its crescendo.

I would prefer not to go into the details, but a year into my job in New York, Jeff, who had brought me into the company as his number two, was let go. All I will say is that he had uncovered certain practices at the company that he vehemently objected to and could not condone. Jeff confided in me what had transpired. As he packed up his personal belongings that day, Jeff pulled me aside and said, "You'll be okay. They need you. They know you are the moneymaker for them. But staying here will probably come at a personal price."

I was devastated. The whirlwind had begun to lift the corners of my roof. I went home to my New York apartment, opened a bottle of my favorite Malbec, poured a glass, and watched the sun disappear over the horizon. Was the sun setting on my New York dream?

As I walked into work the following morning, I knew what I had to do. I would carry on as usual while planning my exit. From what Jeff had told me, I knew I could not stay at the company long term, but here I was, dependent on the company for my livelihood: I lived in a company apartment and I enjoyed a very good income that supported my New York lifestyle. I was certainly conflicted. My principles urged me to quit and walk away; my pragmatic survival instincts told me to sit it out. In the end, I did not have to make the decision: I was fired too! It seemed the owner felt I was too close to Jeff.

But that wasn't the most hurtful part of the whole episode. Almost overnight I went from being surrounded by colleagues and media "friends" who "just *had* to see me" to being met by a disturbing, numbing silence when I reached out to them. I felt so angry and disappointed. Very few of the people from that part of my life remained true friends—not even the group I had traveled with.

As part of my severance package I negotiated a six-month lease in the corporate apartment. I had savings I could draw on. I was fine for a while. I knew I had to find another job, but I was not ready to jump back into the marketing world quite yet. The previous twelve months had been brutal. I was thirty-four and still single, and now unemployed. I wanted to have some fun! But the first thing I wanted to do was spend time with my nephew, so I hopped on a flight and spent a month with my sister.

When I got back to New York, it felt strange not being part of the corporate world. Most of the people I knew were as consumed by their careers as I had been. I slowly began to reconnect with my real friends in the marketing world. One evening just before Christmas, as I was sitting in a wine bar, enjoying a glass of wine with a girlfriend of mine who worked as an anchor at one of the main Spanish TV stations, I finally opened up about how I felt. I wanted the career, I wanted the things that money can buy, but more than anything I really wanted to find the person who was my life partner, who was going to challenge me and who I was going to grow old holding hands with. "Come on. We are going to a party," my friend said. And with that, she grabbed the bill, we grabbed our coats, and we were out on the street hailing a cab.

We got out of the cab on the Lower East Side. It was an area I didn't know at all. It was edgy, artsy, and a little intimidating. My Spanish TV anchor friend walked up to an old brownstone building and without hesitation pushed one of the buttons on the key panel. The door lock buzzed, and we were in. One flight of stairs; with each step the noise grew in volume. At the top of the stairs I could see a door open and a party in full swing. The music was French pop, the lighting was dim, and the atmosphere thick with pot.

"Have fun," my friend said, and disappeared into the throng of people in front of me.

I was still wearing my coat and feeling more than a little self-conscious. I didn't know anyone, and this was definitely not the kind of party I was used to attending in my corporate life. Then suddenly standing next me and gesturing to take my coat was one of the most handsome men I had ever seen.

"Hi, have I seen you before?" It was a corny line, but his charming French accent immediately put me at ease, and I forgave him instantly for his clumsy opening.

His name was Jean-Claude. We chatted most of the evening. I found out that he was just twenty-four years old, ten years younger than me, and from the admiring looks he got, I could see he was on every girl's radar. He had been born in Cannes and was in New York working in his family's jewelry business. As I said goodbye to him at the end of the evening, he slipped me his phone number. I thought to myself that if we got together, I would be a cougar. The thought was certainly not unappealing!

Christmas 2007 was spent with my family in California and playing with my nephew. Jam Jam was growing fast. I was halfway through my six-month corporate apartment lease and beginning to get worried about what would happen when the lease ran out. When I got back to New York, I saw my Spanish TV anchor friend again. I hadn't seen her since she left me at the party.

"So, how was Jean-Claude?" she asked coyly.

"Nice, but I don't think we're right for each other. Bit of an age gap," I said.

"Do you want to see him again?" she asked.

I guess she could tell from my face!

"Yes, you do! He's at Kiss and Fly tonight with his French buddies. Let's go!"

So once more, my friend dragged me across town. This time to the Meatpacking District. Jean-Claude spotted me as soon as we entered the club and I knew the meeting had been prearranged. The sparks flew!

Suddenly I was part of what I like to lovingly call the New York French Mafia circle of restaurateurs. The Meatpacking District in Manhattan became my new stomping ground. Jean-Claude had roommates and his circle of friends became my circle of friends, some of whom are still in my life today. In many ways the New York French Mafia was the anchor I needed at that point in my life. They stopped me from drifting aimlessly. They took me to their parties, they introduced me to the restaurant world. They taught me French. And then there was the passion of having a French lover!

But across town, my lease was up. I had to move out of my corporate apartment. So I rented a small studio apartment close to Madison Square Garden using the dwindling money I had in my savings. I needed to get a job and fast if I were to stay in New York. Meanwhile I continued to see Jean-Claude, but the alarm bells were already ringing about our relationship. Although he worked in his family's business and had an income, I would sometimes find myself paying for him when we went out. I took him to Puerto Rico to see my island and meet my friends. But when he went on vacation back home to Cannes, I was not invited, and he was very secretive about the trip.

Shortly after his return, I found out he had cheated on me while he was away. I ended the relationship right then and there. I knew Jean-Claude was not the person I was going to marry; he was certainly a great distraction, but I was still disappointed with how it ended.

I continued for months to look for a job, but the United States was knee-deep in the biggest global financial crisis since the Great Depression. I tried for several months to find another advertising-marketing opportunity, but nobody was hiring, and people were getting let go across the industry. I managed to stay financially afloat for a while, until things took a turn for the worse at the beginning of 2009. Unable to keep up with my mortgage payments on my apartment in California, I had to let it go and give it back to the bank. I emptied out my 401(k), sold my diamond earrings, bracelets, and Rolex, and hunkered down.

I felt defeated. I had no idea what my next move should be, and while I knew I couldn't stay in the current limbo forever, I was paralyzed. I fell into a temporary depression that took a toll on my weight. I dropped to 105 pounds from my normal weight of 125. I had hit rock bottom for the first time in my life, a humbling and stressful experience. When I had moved to New York two and half years earlier, I never imagined it would end up this way. I was devastated that my dreams were escaping me like sand between my fingers.

I watched *Ellen* and *Oprah* faithfully. I devoured books more often than food. Thanks to Oprah, I didn't lose my sanity. Thanks to her I also discovered *The Secret* by Rhonda Byrne. After I read it the first time, I immediately read it again, and that was when the message clicked. That was when I understood that I was in the presence of a life-changing phenomenon, a different way of living. I was having a major aha moment. It was a new awakening. I latched on to that book and followed it to a T. It helped me ask myself the questions that would later help me visualize my future.

For the first time in my life, I felt like I was going through a midlife crisis. I truly asked myself: *What do I want?* Financial stability was a clear priority, but I vowed to make love my first priority. I didn't want to grow old alone. I desired a partner, an equal, and I didn't want a job that took precedence over love. At thirty-six, after too many years navigating the choppy waters of the dating world, I was able to visualize what I wanted more clearly with the help of *The Secret*. I followed the book's advice to create a vision board that included my future husband's list of attributes: European, different accent than mine, financially stable executive, specifically a banker, wine aficionado, food lover, avid traveler, and music fan who must love to entertain because I sure did, even as a single woman in my shoebox-size Manhattan apartment.

In my eyes, a banker embodied many of the qualities I was looking for in a man. I knew he had to deal with the ups and downs of the global market on a daily basis with clients from around the world, and I admired that. I knew a banker really had to be smart and outgoing, and the lifestyle was a given. I wasn't in it for the money like some of my girlfriends who had their sights set on a hedge fund guy. No: I thrived on having my own career and my own money. I loved the idea of a traditional gentleman with chivalrous qualities who knew how to treat his significant other well. I envisioned an equal partner, someone to exchange ideas with and share certain passions. I had dated a few lawyers but regretfully found them too boring and regimented. All they wanted to do was talk about work—this case, that case. Everything in their lives revolved around a case. *Boring!* I was set up on a blind date with a divorced, childless, narcissistic Wall Street floor trader, but his high-pressure job led to a coke addiction, which didn't fly with me when he mentioned it. I ran away. Nonetheless, bankers intrigued me. I had never dated a banker. Perhaps I would mystify him?

My friends who came to the apartment and saw my vision board called me crazy. They thought I was being unrealistic to add so many details to my vision board, especially when it came to finding love! I turned a deaf ear to their skepticism and continued to firmly believe in the power of putting my wishes out to the universe. During those desperate times, that ray of hope and belief was all I had left, and I wasn't going to let anyone take it away from me.

Oddly, perhaps foolishly enough, the only thing I did not address on that vision board was my health. Since I was feeling fine, I totally took it for granted and forgot to add it to my list of aspirations. Now, there's a lesson if there ever was one on the power of *The Secret*, as I would unfortunately learn just a few years later.

The lease on my apartment was up in March 2009, and I knew I had to swallow my pride. I had no option but to temporarily go back to California to live with my mom and sister and her family. I was crushed and couldn't believe it had come to this, but sometimes we need to get lost in order to find ourselves.

As my Manhattan story seemed to be coming to a close, I visited more and more museums and galleries, cramming them in before I had to leave. From the time I started learning about art when I was a little girl in Puerto Rico, thanks to Fidel, and as I became an adult and traveled the world, I always visited museums and galleries. They were a place of solace for me. Art gave me a sense of comfort; losing myself in a painting was a respite to my day-to-day problems. I also purchased art for myself in all the countries I visited. I really had a passion for it. Plus in New York, I had a girlfriend, Adria, who loved museums, and we each signed up for memberships to two museums a year, so we could have access to four museums and their events between us. We did the same with Broadway shows. We would go almost every month. One month she got the tickets; another month I did. So, when Adria invited me to the Sean Kelly Gallery for an exhibition two weeks before I was due to move back to California, although I wasn't feeling very social, I agreed.

What else did I have going on?

It was opening night of an exhibition of the work of Gavin Turk, a young British artist who was all the rage at the time. My friend and I made the rounds and were social enough. I then stepped to the side to take a moment for myself and concentrate on the art. As I stared into one of Turk's large Jackson Pollock–style paintings, intrigued by his technique and the meaning behind his work, a male voice with a charming foreign accent came up beside me and said, "Some things aren't what they seem at first glance." I turned to find a very attractive man in his forties, dressed sharply in a designer suit and tie, standing to my left and glancing at me with a cheeky grin. "Isn't it amazing," he continued as he looked around the room, "the beauty that surrounds us?"

Who is this guy? I thought as I acknowledged his remark and sized him up. I hadn't noticed him up until that point. Truth be told, he wasn't really my type at first. I was more into the tall, dark, Mediterranean or Middle Eastern types, and this guy was of average height and, judging by his accent, an Englishman in New York. But as we began to chat, his energy enveloped me like a warm blanket; it was just what I needed that evening, when my life was in chaos and turmoil. We talked about art, a natural and effortless exchange. He had good energy that made him incredibly intriguing. We exchanged business cards.

"Oh, you're a banker," I said, thinking about my vision board wishes.

"Yeah. I've been in London but was sent here as an expat for a project a few months ago with my girlfriend," he explained.

Ugh. I couldn't believe he had mentioned the word that every single woman dreads while having a good conversation with a handsome bachelor: *girlfriend*. That was my cue to beat it.

"Oh, well, it was nice to meet you. Have a good evening," I said as we parted ways.

"You too," my new friend said with the warmest of smiles.

"And who was that?" my girlfriend asked with a smile.

"Oh, no one. His name is Nick but he's with someone," I replied wistfully.

Two weeks later I moved back to California. I felt defeated and was completely unaware that I had just met my future husband.

6

Lost and Found

Being deeply loved by someone gives you strength,
while loving someone deeply gives you courage.

—LAO TZU

When I envisioned my life at thirty-six, I never thought I would be living with my family with barely anything to my name besides designer shoes, handbags, clothing, and my health. Jessica was pregnant with her second child and having a difficult pregnancy, so I was happy to be around family. And I was also thrilled that she was expecting a girl. I decided to take this time as a much-needed break to carefully pick up the pieces of what had just happened, in order to think long and hard about how I would need to regain my footing in my life. I needed a rebirth. An improved version of me. Zulema 2.0.

First I had to rebuild my self-esteem. One day as I was chatting over the phone with a girlfriend who worked for a Hispanic lifestyle magazine in New York, she asked unexpectedly, "Would you consider doing a little modeling for the magazine?"

My first reaction was to say no. The experiences of the past year had beaten down my self-confidence, and besides, I never saw myself as a magazine model.

"Think about it," she said. I did think about it and, a month later, I was posing for a bikini shoot for one of their articles and beginning to fall back in love with myself. After accepting that offer, I then began to do a few modeling gigs—all this at the age of thirty-six! Although it may sound superficial or silly, this was actually an important turning point, a lifeline to pull me out of my slump. The experience gave me a purpose and made me stand taller when I walked into a room.

I had been in Orange County for three months, and although I loved living with my family, I yearned to have time to myself and still missed New York. Just as I began to feel the restlessness rising in me, one of my girlfriends from the New York French Mafia invited me to go out there and stay with her and celebrate her birthday. I didn't have the funds to travel, but I did still have my air miles. I booked a ticket and was off to New York. That long weekend was what I needed—another step on the path to rebuilding myself. Being around friends I used to hang out with, who wanted to be with me for who I was and not because of the job I did, was reassuring and comforting. It was on the way back from that weekend that I met Romeo. He restored my faith in men.

Romeo was a very distinguished-looking man: six foot two, Mediterranean skin, salt-and-pepper hair, very George Clooney–like. It sounds like a cliché, but our eyes met as we sat in the American Airlines Admirals Club at JFK waiting for our flights. I was instantly drawn to him. Romeo was Italian-born and spoke Italian, French, and English fluently. As we chatted that day, I learned he was the top executive at one of the world's largest blue chip technology companies. He had traveled the world and visited more places than anyone I knew; he was also divorced and twenty years my senior, with all the wisdom and experience that came with that. He instantly captivated me—class and sexiness rolled into one! Maybe it was the vulnerable situation I found myself in, combined with a strong intellectual and physical attraction I had for him, or the way he treated me, but soon I found myself falling for him.

He made me feel like the sexiest woman in the world, and when I was by his side, I knew I was protected and cared for. But it soon became clear to me that he was not looking for a serious commitment. I don't think deep down he really knew what he wanted from a companion. I wasn't dead-set on having kids back then, but that was something he had already done. He made it clear he didn't want to start a family. I couldn't fathom being with someone who took that option off the table completely. I was in my mid-thirties. I wasn't ready to shut that door just yet. Who knows what would have happened if I had not been so steadfast about this. My story might have been quite different.

I vividly remember the last time we were together. My Spirit guide told me it would be our last time. We never spoke about our relationship ending, but we both knew that, although we cared for each other deeply, we were not meant to be a long-term match. I have often thought to myself, *Wow, what if I had met him when I was five years older, when I knew better what I really wanted out of life and my partner?* Throughout our time together I wanted to tell him how much I cared for him but always stopped short of doing so, out of fear he would reject me. He would have been so speechless.

And so, as we left the Four Seasons suite we had shared for several days in San Francisco, I held on to him a little longer at our goodbye kiss. I didn't want it to end, but I knew it was going to. He would always live in my heart as a very special person who touched my life deeply and meaningfully.

About a year later I was shopping at Bloomingdale's in SoHo, stopped by at the second-floor restaurant for a snack, and heard Romeo's voice. It wasn't my imagination. He was sitting with a woman, clearly a love interest, smiling, laughing, and flirting. My heart froze. I didn't have the guts to interrupt and say hi. I had nothing to say. Instead I ran away as quickly as I could because I didn't want him to see me. We had spent such intimate moments together. He had helped build Zulema 2.0. At that moment I had never been so close to yet so distant from someone I cared for and, if I was honest, still missed. I was crushed. I had never considered getting back together with any of my previous beaus, but I knew that if I had the chance, I would have given it another go with Romeo. I needed to trust the timing in my life.

The start of true love began in September 2009, on a day like any other, as I was checking my email. There it was: one short message that would change everything.

Oh, wow, he remembered me was my initial reaction as I clicked open the email to read a note from the coy Englishman I had met six months earlier at the Sean Kelly Gallery. Nick was writing to let me know that he was newly single. He had broken up with his girlfriend and was wondering if I'd be up for grabbing a drink in the city. Amused by this surprising turn of events, I explained that although I currently lived in California, I was actually hoping to be in New York toward the end of that month. Sadly, he was scheduled to be in London, so the meeting would have to wait.

What occurred after this initial exchange were some very amusing emails. We were clearly intrigued by one another, very curious, and also somewhat cautious, given the distance between us. Yet, as our sporadic and excitable bursts of digital communication became more frequent, it wasn't long before we were corresponding daily, and emails turned into phone calls a few months later. By December 2009 all that was left was for me and Nick to meet again. Think *Sex and the City* meets *You've Got Mail*.

Unlike any other man I had met, I never felt any skepticism toward Nick. In fact, I liked him so much—so much more than I can say—that I actually never told anyone about him. I wanted to keep this feeling private, because it felt special and different than any of the other connections I'd had with men in the past. Plus I kept thinking, *This can't really be happening. This perfect guy that checks off all the boxes of what I want in a partner couldn't have just been dropped in my lap.* I kept waiting for the other shoe to drop, but it didn't happen, instead just easy, witty conversation as we got to know each other.

I think my relationship with Nick got off to such a strong start because we had the rare opportunity to actually get to know each other profoundly before any physical interactions took place. And in that unique space in time, our love slowly began to blossom. There is a physical element to attraction, of course; that is undeniable. Yet the way Nick communicated with me, and the life he led, oozed sexiness and charm. Every anecdote he shared revealed another part of him that made me like him even more. I didn't see any obstacles. I didn't have any preconceived notions. I didn't judge. I was genuinely open to love, and love with him. One day it dawned on me: I felt like I'd just met a real-life James Bond straight from my vision board! Hello, *The Secret*. Thank you to my guardian angel and to Papi. It was easy to picture us together because I'd practically manifested him! There was so much more I wanted to explore in real life.

I was actually planning a second trip to New York in December, but when I mentioned this to Nick, he said he had to be in Canada that weekend. I remember thinking, *Wow, this guy is never home. Is this something I really want?* In all honesty, I figured he was probably dating other women. There was nothing I could do or say at that point, as we had yet to meet, and I was still enjoying the company of my noncommittal Italian, so I didn't bring it up either. Even so, my communication with Nick felt special, as did he, and I didn't want to ruin it. I wanted to see where it would go.

A pivotal moment in our relationship came on New Year's Eve 2009. Nick was in London for the holidays, and I was at a girlfriend's home in West Hollywood. After going out to dinner with friends, rather than staying out to ring in the New Year, Nick hurried home, called me, and welcomed the year with me on the phone. As the annual countdown reached midnight, we finally set a date to meet again in person: January 13, 2010.

Ten months after first crossing paths at the gallery exhibition in New York, I was packing my suitcase to fly across the country for my first date with Nick, the man who had serendipitously come into my life. Our chemistry was about to be tested.

I arrived in New York a couple of days early to stay with a friend and his wife in Chelsea, the only two people in whom I had confided the real purpose behind this trip. I was excited and nervous, like a teen who was finally going out with the boy she had harbored a crush on for months.

The day of our date, I set the afternoon aside to get ready.

I paid special attention to my hair, went for a natural makeup look, slipped into a black bodycon Dolce & Gabbana dress, accessorized with a black velvet belt that enhanced my waist and curves, carried a fur in hand, wore peep-toe Louboutins, and then walked outside with my head high, hailed a cab, and set off for the Thompson Hotel in SoHo. As I made my way there, I prayed to my dad and God to guide and protect me.

Nick and I met at the bar, followed by dinner at Kittichai, which at that time was the hotel's Thai restaurant. When he suggested this spot, I thought it was the weirdest coincidence because Jean-Claude had taken me to that same restaurant two years earlier on *our* first date. And stranger yet: we were seated at the same table! What were the odds? I wasn't sure what this meant, but I decided to accept and welcome it as sign of good things to come. (*The Secret* hadn't let me down yet.)

When I arrived at the hotel a little late, I wondered if I'd recognize Nick. My heart was pounding in an excited and nervous way. Sure enough, the dapper British gentleman who had felt like a figment of my imagination was in front of me, live and in the flesh. We hugged, gave each other a quick kiss, and exchanged pleasantries.

"So nice to see you," I said.

"Oh, wow, you look amazing," he replied, grabbing my hand.

He pulled out the chair for me; I sat down and looked across the table into his kind eyes. My heart bounced. It was our first in-person conversation in ten months. Someone pinch me, please! We skipped over the usual first date chatter. Right away, the conversation became up-close and personal, and the moment was as intimate as ever. As for the chemistry question? It was palpable. I breathed a quiet sigh of relief, and for the first time in my life that little voice inside said, *OK, this is it. He's the one.*

And then I thought to myself, *Zulema, don't mess it up.*

I knew I had to exercise restraint with Nick, because I truly was interested in him for a serious relationship. I needed to take it slow. I refused to sweep in and take control of the situation, as I had so often done on previous dates when the guy showed any sign of indecisiveness or weakness. When it was time to order, I told Nick what I wanted, and when he ordered for me like a gentleman, I was all in. This guy knew what he was doing.

Nick was the real deal.

Overall, the date was perfect. Our meal was on point, the conversation was enthralling, sparks were flying, and my heart couldn't stop smiling. When we finished the main course and the waiter asked if we were interested in seeing the dessert menu, Nick immediately replied, "No, thank you." Then he turned to me and said, "I hope you don't mind, but I have a better idea. How about we go back to my place, which is not that far from here, to have dessert there? I have a bottle of Dom Pérignon 1982 in the fridge." *Oh, man,* I thought. *I'm in trouble.* He clearly remembered my wild obsession with champagne . . . *Well played, Nick, well played.* I couldn't say no to my favorite poison and more time together. So off we went.

As we walked over to his place, my instincts grew louder and louder, and kept telling me over and over, *Zulema, you cannot sleep with him on the first date. This guy is meant for something serious. Don't mess it up. Just go, have dessert and Dom Pérignon, and leave.* Even so, our mutual attraction went far beyond my control. But against my better judgment, I spent the night. Gah! I could hardly resist!

The next morning, as Nick got ready for work, I slipped back into my walk-of-shame outfit, thinking, *Holy shit, Zulema, what have you done? You're never going to see him again!* What I didn't realize was that it wasn't really our first date, but more like our hundredth. We'd practically been dating for about four months, long-distance.

Nick and I left the apartment together to hop on the Canal Street 1 train uptown. My stop was Thirty-Fourth Street; his was Times Square. As the doors slid open, we said our good-byes with a quick, romantic kiss—a good sign, I thought!—and I prayed and visualized seeing him again. The previous night he had mentioned possibly having dinner together on Friday, but I knew all too well that many guys uttered such feel-good sentiments, never to follow through with them later. Not Nick! I went along with my day, tangled up in deep and exhilarating flashbacks from the night before, and then, to my relief, a text came through and later a call from him.

I know it sounds cliché, but that day I knew that Nick would be my future husband—the man I had visualized on my vision board a year and a half earlier. I had waited patiently, and here he was. Thank you, universe. Thank you, Papi. Thank you, Guardian Angel! Never in my romantic life did I feel such serenity and certainty over a choice.

Nick and I saw each other every day that week. He joined my New York French Mafia friends for dinner at Fig & Olive in the Meatpacking District on Friday, and afterward we all went dancing at Kiss & Fly. He made a solid first impression on my friends. I stayed over. The next night, after spending the day with my *abuela* Esperanza in the Bronx, Nick and I came up with our life list on our third date at Dylan Prime. We included all the grand experiences and memories we planned to have and make together over the course of our life together. It seemed both presumptuous and refreshingly open at the same time. Who has the nerve to commit to a lifetime of special moments on a third date? Nick and I did, which is exactly why we knew from the beginning that we had something special.

We spent that Sunday night with Nick's colleagues at a corporate suite at Madison Square Garden watching a Rangers game, and a few days later we had our sixth date to celebrate my thirty-seventh birthday. After yet another *supercalifragilisticexpialidocious* evening, we went back to Nick's place. He poured Dom Pérignon 1990 in Baccarat flutes and brought them over to the sofa where I was sitting. He turned on his Naim system to play a song that he said reminded him of us, John Mayer's "Comfortable." Then he stared into my eyes and said, "I love you."

Although these were three words every girl longs to hear, was this all happening a little too soon? I'll admit that I was a bit overwhelmed by our intense in-person connection over the past few days, and most definitely had powerful feelings for Nick, but I couldn't say "I love you" in return. The most I could muster was "I really, really like you." I didn't have doubts about Nick, but I just wasn't ready to commit to those words so soon in our relationship. I was so used to men who took their time and played games. Nick's openness and vulnerability was refreshing, but I wasn't prepared to trust in them fully. What if I returned the sentiment and he changed his mind? I had been guided by a higher intuition that had led me to Nick. Exactly what I had envisioned and asked of the universe was happening. This was a first ever. However, I wanted to still tread lightly.

Two days later I flew back to California. Nick hopped on

a plane to London. After sleeping in his arms for seven days straight, leaving New York City was heart-wrenching. All I wanted was to fall asleep with his arms wrapped around me, safe and protected. Aside from our life list, we hadn't made any concrete future plans. But we did know that we were both committed to making this relationship work, the distance between us be damned.

Our daily calls, texts, and emails continued with aching hearts that yearned to be together. During one of our calls near the end of January, the conversation turned serious. "If this is ever going to work, you're going to have to come here," Nick said, "because I can't move my life, my job, and my career to California." I was initially startled by his forthrightness, but Nick was right. I had occasional freelance gigs on the West Coast but nothing permanent to keep me there. We decided then and there that I should move in with him. It was the first time in my life that I would live with a man and not have my own place.

When I told Mami, she was shocked, asked too many questions about my mystery man—remember, I had kept him a secret from almost everyone for fear that it would jinx our bond—and wished me all the best. In other words, she approved. Less than a month after our first official date, I flew to New York.

7

Love in the Time of Chaos

Chaos is inherent in all compounded things.
Strive on with diligence.

—BUDDHA

My relationship with Nick almost ended as quickly as it began.

When the wheels touched down at JFK on a red-eye from LAX, I felt it was a new beginning for me. I was on cloud nine when I caught a glimpse of Nick waiting for me in the arrivals area. He gave me a big hug and a romantic kiss. However, it worried me that Nick looked like he hadn't slept all night. I felt something in the air that I had not experienced with him before: a kind of distance that felt greater than the miles that had kept us apart. Nick blamed his quiet demeanor on having been up the night before preparing the apartment for my arrival. My gut said there was more to this story, but I didn't push.

Nick had taken the day off from work to be with me. The moment we arrived at his apartment, our rapport normalized. We fell into each other's arms with our passion outweighing our initially awkward reunion. Then we showered, grabbed a late brunch, and came back to rest. I still had this feeling that something was off. Nick was subdued. I was confused but avoided saying anything, and we went to bed early.

The next morning, before heading to work, Nick showed me to my closet. I unpacked as it snowed outside. It was the kind of wintry and peaceful New York afternoon when the snow muffles the sounds of the busy streets.

When Nick came home from work, he still seemed off to me. I asked him if something was wrong.

"Oh, nothing, no, I'm fine," he said.

"Is it that this is too much for you, having me here?" I asked.

"I don't know, I need time to think," he replied.

I stared back at him, speechless. As I probed around to get to the bottom of the issue, a gazillion thoughts ran through my mind. Mami's voice repeated itself over and over: "You trust too much." I asked myself how my intuition could be so far off as to think this was the man for me when he could do this to me.

After dinner at a neighborhood restaurant, our mood was somber. I was downright sad. Back at the apartment, Nick sat me down on the sofa and, after a long pause, said, "Actually, the more I think about this, the more I realize that I don't think I can make this work. I'm uncomfortable. I can't have you here . . . I think you need to go."

Just like that, an out-of-the-blue, under-the-belt blow. The air was driven from my lungs. I could hardly breathe. What was happening? With a gush of tears streaming down my face, I glared at him in disbelief. The guy who insisted that I move across the country to be with him now had the nerve, less than twenty-four hours after my arrival, to kick me out—into a blizzard, no less? My mind raced. Nick retired to his room while I, sobbing, shattered, and heartbroken, ducked into the other bedroom to call my girlfriend Isabel.

"I don't know what to do," I cried. "I have nowhere to go."

"Stay in that room and lock the door," she insisted. "You don't really know this guy. He could be a psycho and try to kill you while you're sleeping!"

Isabel scared me straight. After all, she could be right! I thought about how I barely knew Nick, and for all I knew, maybe the universe had gotten this wrong: maybe it had confused my vision board with a most wanted list! Feelings of devastation, loss, and doubt about my instincts and judgment got the best of me. I spent my second night back in New York locked in a room, all by myself, crying my heart out all night. Nick could hear me because my crying was deep and uncontrollable.

When morning came, I gathered myself and walked into the living room to find Nick there waiting for me. "I booked a room for you at the W Hotel on Forty-Ninth Street and Lexington," he said matter-of-factly. "I'll reimburse you for your flight and send your boxes back to California as soon as they arrive."

Shell-shocked, I uttered, "That's the least you can do!"

"Of course," he replied calmly.

I cried inconsolably as I packed the stuff I had put away just a day earlier while Nick worked from his home office. When I was ready, still wearing his gentleman's cap, he called a car service and shipped me off to my hotel. When I arrived there, I was hurt and fuming. I called my closest aunt, Ramona, who lives in Virginia, and she immediately said, "Why don't you come here for a few days? It's closer than California. You can decompress while you figure out your next move." I agreed, but I had to remain in the city for three more days due to the blizzard that had grounded all flights until further notice. I spent the next three days locked up in my hotel room crying, watching bad TV, and ordering room service but unable to eat as the snow blanketed the streets outside my window. I kept thinking of how romantic it would have been to spend those snow days with Nick in his apartment. Suddenly it dawned on me that there must be something major causing him to behave in such a weird way. It was so uncharacteristic. Was there another woman? Did he get fired from work?

My crying did not stop once I finally landed in Virginia. What made this man suddenly transform into Mr. Hyde? What had I done to offend him? Had he never really loved me? I was in pain. I also had a nagging thought in my mind that I simply couldn't let go of: *There has to be another explanation. Something else must be going on to make him act like that.* I was determined to get to the bottom of whatever had turned Nick around so abruptly. So, against everyone's advice, I sent him an email:

First and foremost, what you've done is horrific. Second of all, I want the truth. I deserve the truth. What you just did to me is cruel. Please tell me what's going on. It can't be something I did. This is on you.

Two days went by with no response, and then came the answer I suspected to be true:

I have a big personal issue that I can't tell you about. I am in London. Will contact you upon returning.

Suspicions confirmed, at least in part. I flew back to New York for a few days. Then, I went to Puerto Rico to spend some time with one of my best friends. I desperately needed to clear my mind. That's when Nick reached out to me again:

I'm very sorry. This was not my intention at all, but I have a big personal situation and because of it, I am in no position to engage in any type of relationship at the time being.

I had no idea what he was talking about, but of course I needed to know more.

Well, why don't you just tell me what the problem is? You're assuming that I can't handle it, and that's not fair to either of us.

After some back and forth, Nick finally cracked. We decided to meet in person for cocktails the following week. I was nervous about meeting him. Despite what had happened, I was excited to see him and was willing to forgive him if he offered a good reason. But first I needed him to come clean with the truth. So I went with an open mind and heart.

Over a bottle of Krug champagne, Nick revealed that the day before I was scheduled to arrive, he received a desperate call from his ex-wife telling him that their youngest son, Charles, would be on a flight to New York the following week and moving in with him because she "no longer knew what to do with him." He was now Nick's responsibility. Regretfully, Charles had a drug problem, had failed his exams, and had been asked to leave his school. Nick's ex had shifted the problem to him.

Everything snapped into place for me. *No wonder* Nick had been so far removed when he picked me up at the airport! His son had suddenly become his life's priority, and he instantly assumed I'd want nothing to do with it. He didn't think it was fair to bring me into it. He believed I deserved better. He was willing to put his own happiness on hold to help his son.

"Really?" I asked, somewhat amazed. "*That's* the problem? *That's* why you pushed me out? It's not because of another woman?" I went on to explain that I had already dealt with a similar scenario many years earlier with Jonathan. I had had to navigate the aftermath of his divorce and help him figure out how to help his eldest son break his drug addiction. This was not my first rodeo, no matter how foreign it might be to most women. Nick was so relieved to hear this. His voice immediately softened, and he hugged me tightly.

Nick and I decided together that we would give our relationship another go, regardless of these unforeseen circumstances, and simply hope for the best. We both deserved to find love and knew we were meant to be together. To quit, we realized, would be cowardice. The following Saturday, Nick introduced me to his son Charles over dinner at Nobu. Nick explained to his son that he would like to have me move back in and that we wanted to be together. By the end of February, I transitioned back to Nick's Tribeca penthouse—this time for good.

Come March, Nick, Charles, and I flew to London to meet Nick's parents and his eldest son, John. I also met one of Nick's best friends and his entire team at Morgan Stanley. We then shared our first trip as a family to Austria, where we spent thirteen days skiing.

The first eleven months of my relationship with Nick were an uphill battle—far from stereotypical cohabitation bliss—and full of both highs and lows, ups and downs. But what always prevailed was our desire to be with each other no matter what outside chaotic circumstance came our way. While we fought tooth and nail to keep our romance going, Charles was always our priority. I also took it upon myself to teach this eighteen-year-old a few life basics while he was under our roof, like how to use a washer and dryer, cook, clean, wash his bedsheets every week, and a few personal hygiene tips. It would have been a disservice to Charles to let him zone out in front of the TV all day. I also encouraged him to enroll in a program at Huntington Learning Center to get his GED. Hats off to Charles, because he nailed the GED with a perfect score in math. The kid was good with numbers, just like his father. A few months later he was accepted and enrolled at Pace University.

I'm not going to lie: those first few months with Charles were extremely rough on my relationship with Nick. He and I had different views about what it meant to parent, and I was in an awkward position to have the authority to express my opinions but did not yet have the title of *stepmom* or children of my own to use as anecdotes or examples. Keep in mind, too, that we weren't just bickering over normal parenting stuff, like whether Charles needed a curfew or if we should add more chores to his household duties. We were talking about how to parent a teenager who was battling a drug problem. I also grew up Catholic, with strict rules and responsibilities to keep me in check. I had opinions rooted in these values.

So much tension in the air didn't exactly pair well with a kinky love life. Living with Nick's son under the same roof meant no spur-of-the-moment sex, no walking around naked, no lying in on a Sunday morning without a care in the world, no long nights out for fear that leaving him alone would trigger a relapse, no traveling—and one-on-one dates as a couple were few and far between. I wanted Nick's son to thrive and achieve, and because I deeply loved Nick, I was willing to do anything for him. If we spent the rest of our lives together as we had planned, I knew this wouldn't be the only challenge that would come our way. The good news was Charles slowly regained control of himself and his life, which eventually allowed months of stress to shift from Nick's shoulders and give us breathing room.

Nick's fiftieth birthday was at the end of the year, and I volunteered to throw him a fabulous party. When we first met, he had mentioned that nobody had ever thrown him a birthday party before. Given my event planning skills from my marketing and advertising days, I orchestrated the party of a lifetime for over a hundred people at the newly opened SoHi space at the now Dominick hotel. The stunning panoramic views from the forty-sixth floor were only surpassed by the stunned look on Nick's face. We watched a video from Nick's older son, John, projected onto a big screen at the front of the room. John wished Nick a happy birthday and apologized for not being there in person. Nick was happy to see it, even if he missed his son. But then he got a tap on the shoulder and turned around to see John standing behind him: I had flown John in for the evening as a surprise!

Charles went off to college as the new year rolled in, and my relationship with Nick entered a new phase. We officially felt that we could let down our guard and act like a "normal" couple. We had ticked off a few things from our life list while Charles was with us: a romantic sunset helicopter tour of Manhattan, a private Six Flags VIP Magic Mountain visit to ride all the rides without waiting in line, and meeting John Mayer. The jaunts were fun and there was much more to do. Now we could dive in feet and hearts first!

We began ticking off items on our list with gusto. Skydiving was a big one for us. One of Nick's fiftieth-birthday gifts was a skydiving experience for the two of us. So, one Saturday, on a beautiful spring morning, we took a car ride out to Long Island to a skydiving center. After a classroom briefing, equipment fitting, and the mildly disturbing experience of signing an indemnity release in case of our death, we were walking across the grass to board a twin-engine prop plane to whisk us off to the skies. As the plane reached 12,500 feet, the door was pulled open and a massive wind rush slapped my face. Strapped to my instructor, he shouted above the noise of the wind to shuffle forward along the bench we were sitting on toward the open door. And suddenly there I was, sitting on the edge of the plane, with my legs dangling outside, looking down at the ground so far below. I felt a burst of panic sweep over me and then, "One, two, three, jump." Well, I didn't actually jump, the instructor pushed us out of the plane. Falling upside down at first, I saw the plane growing quickly smaller as we began our rapid descent. The panic grew stronger. I was totally out of control. And then my instructor skillfully maneuvered us so I was the one facing forward watching the ground rush toward me. At that moment, I felt like a bird, soaring through the air at 120 miles per hour. My panic turned to exhilaration. I didn't want the moment to end. But in no time the stick figures on the ground turned into easily recognizable people, our parachute opened, and we gently descended the last few thousand feet to the ground.

I thanked God I was alive. I thanked God for letting us

cross off this life list together. I know it is our mind and fears that often get in our own way and make things appear more daunting or insurmountable than they actually are. I compared the moment of jumping off the plane to the challenges and chaos I've often experienced and felt in my life. Sometimes finding myself spinning out of control and then finding an inner calm and stability. Not being in control of the situation was unnerving; I couldn't control our leaping out of the plane, the parachute opening, or landing. I would not have done it had I not fully trusted my instructor. Just like I realized, how I couldn't overcome life's obstacles without trusting my life partner. And lastly, it reinforced, yet again, that while others might think you may be crazy, irresponsible, or reckless, I am not swayed by others' opinions or criticism and do what I want to do. Stepping out of my comfort zone and forging my own individual path is a better way to live than just settling for what others expect you to do.

Shortly after our skydiving trip, I was hit with more medical mysteries. I received a call that I had an irregular mammogram and needed a biopsy of calcifications in my breasts. The news was nothing too alarming. I would need to monitor them closely from then on.

The bigger sucker punch came when I began having issues with hair loss, abrupt hot and cold body temperature changes, quick weight gain for no apparent reason, and an unquenchable thirst. While undergoing a heart stress test, I was referred to an endocrinologist, who ordered a thyroid sonogram. It was then that I was diagnosed with my first official autoimmune disease.

"You have an enlarged thyroid and nodules on your thyroid, which may signal Hashimoto's disease," the doctor said. "Have you ever been treated for hypothyroidism?"

The question instantly made me flash back to my late twenties. I had been diagnosed with hypothyroidism by my primary care physician and was put on a very low dose of thyroid therapy. However, about a year later, my thyroid levels were normal, the doctor took me off the medication, and we called it a day. I thought that what I had suffered was temporary, never imagining it was still active in my body. Of course my thyroid levels returned to normal when I had the thyroid treatment in my twenties: it meant the medicine was working. I later learned that having hypothyroidism and letting it go untreated for so many years was a serious mistake and allowed the disease to continue to progress. I was now paying the price for those years of neglect.

I was certainly exhibiting all the symptoms of hypothyroidism, and my endocrinologist asked, "Do you suffer from constipation? That can be one of the major effects."

I thought back to all of the health problems I had had while I was working at The Bravo Group and my struggles to get to work some days because of severe constipation.

The endocrinologist put me on a low dose of Synthroid and said, "No more gluten for you."

This was my first major dietary restriction since my gallbladder had been removed more than fifteen years earlier. The doctor also diagnosed me with osteopenia, which is a lighter form of osteoporosis, meaning that I had lower bone density, I was more prone to fractures, and surgical healing times would be extra long and complex, especially if it was related to a bone-related procedure. Welcome to my late thirties! Health issues were starting to become a part of my life. I would need a bone density test every two years.

During the previous November, I decided it was time to get

back into the workforce. I had loved my advertising and marketing career and missed the everyday challenges and achievements it brought to my life, so when Telemundo offered me a consultant position on their marketing and integrated marketing team to specifically work on the L'Oréal account, I accepted in a heartbeat. This would mark my first job on the media side of marketing, and I was thrilled.

I set up my own marketing and consulting company, ready to hit the ground running. However, what I thought would be a steady, rewarding first assignment turned into a breathless marathon with grueling hours and constant chaos. I did my best to help support the account, but despite working four days at the company's offices, Fridays from home, and endless long nights, I was not getting anywhere. Worse still, my boss oozed negativity from her pores. It seemed to me that she carried an incredible amount of anger at the world, at people, and at me. So, for the second time, I had to put up with an antagonistic boss, this time a woman. One morning at 6:30 a.m., as I was getting out of the car that had taken me home after working twenty-four hours straight, finalizing a critical media campaign for the client. I got a call from my boss. "The client is not happy. *I* am not happy. We need to make some revisions urgently. I need you back in the office."

I'll never forget the look on Nick's face when I showed up in the bedroom to tell him that the car was waiting for me downstairs and I was going to shower and go back to the office. Nick was very unhappy with how I was being treated and was concerned for my health. The job was far from what I had expected, but I was determined to make it work—until my health began to act up again that winter.

Nick and I had taken off to the Banyan Tree Mayakoba resort on the Riviera Maya with my beloved friend Lisa and her husband during Presidents' Day weekend for a much-needed break. Even in the gorgeous Mexican sunshine, I spent most of those days feeling terrible. At every meal, after a few bites of food my stomach would swell up to abnormal proportions to the point that I couldn't push myself to swallow another mouthful of anything. I would put my best foot forward, smile through the discomfort, and assume I had caught a traveler's stomach bug. But when the symptoms continued after our return and into the next month, I couldn't deny that something was very wrong. I could barely get any food down because it would give me excruciating stomach pain, and when I forced myself to eat, I would immediately vomit. As a result, I lost fifteen pounds without even trying.

One day, while Nick was on a business trip to London, I texted him in despair, "I feel so unwell. I'm in so much pain. I don't know what's going on, but I have to go to the ER."

That was the first of four trips to the ER in one month, all of which were futile. Each time the doctor put me through the same array of tests, X-rays, MRIs, and blood work, and each time the doctor came back without concrete results and a slightly frustrated and concerned look on his face. "Everything looks okay," he or she would say. "We don't know what you have."

If the doctors didn't know, you can imagine how hopeless I felt. I didn't think the issue had to do with my IBS, because I recognized that what I felt was a different type of pain—one that was located in the top half of my torso, closer to my stomach. By this time I had stopped eating solid food and the constant vomiting reminded me that my mom used to tell me I would projectile vomit as a newborn with pyloric stenosis.

I saw a gastroenterologist, who concluded that I was likely battling a motility issue with my digestive system. He suspected the food I ate wasn't being properly broken down. However, this doctor wanted to rule out any other type of virus or parasite I might have caught while in Mexico. Once I was in the clear for that—thank God my belly was free of bugs—he decided to test my digestive system with a gastric empty study. This is a nuclear test that can only be conducted in a hospital and normally takes from three to five hours. I was fed a delicious combination of egg white scramble and radioactive material, which would then be detected and recorded by an X-ray of my abdomen to monitor how long it took for the food to pass through my digestive tract. The test took *eight hours*. The food became trapped in my stomach and just didn't want to budge.

Upon reviewing the study results, the gastroenterologist explained, "It looks like you have a medical condition called gastroparesis, a partial stomach paralysis that prevents your stomach from emptying in a typical fashion; as a result, food sits inside your stomach for an abnormally long time."

This was why just a few bites of food made me nauseated. He went on to say that my vagus nerve, which is responsible for the stomach contractions that move food to the small intestine, was more than likely damaged. The longer food remained in my stomach undigested, the more likely bacteria would multiply, which could also eventually cause a condition called leaky gut or small intestinal bacteria overgrowth (SIBO), which damages the lining of the small intestine and causes undigested food particles, toxic waste, and bacteria to seep through and enter the bloodstream. Common causes of gastroparesis are diabetes (which I don't have, although it is rampant in my family) and stress (which I had loads of while working at Telemundo). It is an uncommon and incurable condition. The only drug that can treat gastroparesis had still not been approved by the FDA at the time, so it wasn't available in the United States. All the doctor could offer me as a solution to my stomach nightmare was the advice to reduce stress, adjust my diet to avoid foods high in fiber, restrict my intake of solids and fat, and eat very small meals throughout the day. Anything more would exacerbate my symptoms.

I took notes at every doctor's appointment, since it was all so overwhelming and unfamiliar. I had such a huge fear of what would happen to me that I conducted my own research, talked to doctor friends of mine, and refused to accept what doctors said as the final word. This is a frame of mind that became my standard operating procedure with each new diagnosis I received. When I learned that domperidone (sounds like Dom Pérignon, the champagne—how's that for irony!), the drug that can treat this disorder wasn't available in the United States (it is now, but with restricted access), was sold in the United Kingdom, I got my hands on a box, since Nick traveled to London frequently. Unfortunately, it didn't work for me, so dietary changes and restrictions were my only hope. (If only the cure was Dom Pérignon! I know that works!)

At this point I quit my job, stayed home, and lived on a mostly liquid diet for the next three months. I lost thirty pounds in the process. It was a very debilitating and agonizing period in my life. To add to the stress, none of my friends or family understood what I had because no one had ever heard of this illness and kept asking questions I didn't have answers for, or were outright skeptical of my condition. The only person in my life who understood what I was going through was Nick.

I went from savoring every dish put in front of me to dreading every bite of food that went into my stomach. There were many days when Nick and I would go out to a restaurant and I would just watch him eat because I couldn't. When staying over at a friend's house and seeing that I was not eating very much, our hosts would continually ask whether I had enough to eat and suggest I try this or that, despite the fact that I made it clear I could not eat three meals a day. They were only trying to be good hosts, but I found it exhausting and frustrating.

On April 15, 2012, a gloriously sunny spring Sunday, Nick and I stopped for brunch at Dylan Prime, our favorite neighborhood restaurant and site of our third date. He ordered steak and eggs. I got a salad. We were super excited, because we were on the verge of closing on our first apartment together as a couple: a stunning space in Tribeca, a new-construction duplex penthouse that was just two blocks from where we lived. After visiting the sales gallery to choose the finishes and hardware, we began to talk decorating before Nick changed the subject.

"Well, now that we're going to have a home together," he said, smiling, "I think it would be the ideal time for me to ask you this." He grabbed my hands, moved closer to me on the bench where we were sitting, and with the sweetest look on his face, radiating happiness, said:

"I want to spend the rest of my life with you, Zulema. I love you and I just can't see myself without you by my side. Do you want to marry me?"

What the huh?

Let's just say that Nick caught me so off guard that I glanced up at him, puzzled, and said, "What? What are you *talking* about?"

"Well," he laughed, "I'm asking you if you want to get married."

"Wait a minute. Are you proposing to me?" I asked, completely taken aback.

"Yes, I'm proposing to you," he said.

"I don't believe you," I said.

"I'm serious," he insisted.

"I don't *believe* you," I repeated, flabbergasted.

He smiled. "Honey," he said, "I'm being serious."

Then Nick kissed me passionately. I felt it. That feeling of happy goose bumps from head to toe invaded my body.

"Okay," I said, half joking and half daring, "if you're being serious, then pick up the phone and call Mami and my family right now and tell them."

With that, Nick reached over to my side of the table, grabbed my iPhone, dialed my mom's number, and shared the incredible news. If you can believe it, only then did I think that Nick was telling me truthfully that he wanted to marry me. The waterworks began to flow and I cried on and off for the next four hours. Yes, four hours. I just couldn't believe this day had finally come. After everything we'd been through, the man who I felt was the One since our first date was actually now taking the step to become the *official* One! I was finally engaged at thirty-nine years old.

I had once casually said that it would be nice to get married by the time I was forty, which now was only a year away. Otherwise the nickname my family called me after turning thirty—"Jamona," the Puerto Rican term for *spinster*—would turn from joke to reality. The prospect of becoming Mrs. Nick Farley made me feel I'd won the lottery. I had an overwhelming sense of happiness and was officially off the market to any man who would look my way.

Nick said he had been thinking about proposing for some

time, especially after seeing how I had helped his son thrive, which he felt spoke volumes about me and demonstrated how much I loved him. But he wanted his proposal to be done in a private, low-key way—not a big, showy event. He had caught me off guard, but it couldn't have been better. I was never a believer in the get-down-on-one-knee kind of marriage proposal, maybe because I read too much into the man having to kneel down in front of the woman. I saw my husband as my equal, on the same playing field as me.

To me, the whole moment was perfect. This was the happiest day of my life. The only thing missing was an engagement ring. Nick said he had thought about choosing a ring for me but sensed that I would have my own idea of what I wanted and decided we should choose it together. I was so glad that I always listened to Spirit and never ended up marrying young to someone I would later regret being with. I had met my share of fascinating fellows; each of those experiences had given me the insight to know what I wanted in my partner and how to allow myself to be loved by the right man when he came along. I had followed my heart, my intuition, and my own path to finally discover the partner of a lifetime—for better or worse, in sickness and in health.

On May 17, 2013, on a Tribeca rooftop, as the sun set, with the Manhattan skyline behind us, I married the love of my life.

8

Wedding Bliss

Our honeymoon will shine our life long; its beams
will only fade over your grave or mine.
—CHARLOTTE BRONTË, *JANE EYRE*

Our wedding day was out of this world. It looked like a fake backdrop, too perfect to be real. There was not a cloud in the sky, in contrast to the storm that had swept through the day before. The sun enveloped Manhattan in its warm and radiant light, which I took to be a blessing from God and my father that my soon-to-be husband and I were off to a blessed start. As I stood at the altar staring into the kind blue eyes of the dapper British gentleman before me, I would have never imagined how important this commitment would be, given our future ahead.

For so many years I had chosen to put career before love, love before marriage, in contrast to what my Puerto Rican culture dictates or what many of my friends had done. I wasn't going to marry the wrong man to avoid becoming a spinster and I didn't want to get married for marriage's sake. I always intended to find the man I would grow old with, the one whose hand I would hold until the end, the one who would be the Mark Antony to my Cleopatra. Some—namely, Mami and my gossipy friends—might say it took longer than expected, but our paths crossed when they were meant to and led us to the moment it did. Standing on a rooftop that overlooked the Hudson and the Statue of Liberty, I couldn't think of pledging my devotion to anyone in my past, present, or imagination but Nick.

As my own wedding designer and planner, I took an entire year to plan our wedding to my heart's content, making sure every last detail was exactly as I wanted it to be. Because I had never done this before, I hired a real wedding planner to work with me through the year so she could bring my vision to life on our wedding day. Nick and I had one overarching goal in mind: we wanted our union to be a one-of-a-kind feast and party that would remain forever etched in everyone's minds—and we succeeded.

For our wedding venue, we chose a space called the Tribeca Rooftop, which gave us a gorgeous outdoor space for the sunset ceremony and an indoor space for the formal dinner and party. After all, my first date with Nick took place only a few blocks away, we began living together in that same neighborhood, and we got engaged at a restaurant only steps from this location.

Nick and I desired a lavish affair right out of a James Bond movie—especially since I often told Nick that he was my own James Bond. This became the theme of our wedding. Elegance was the priority. We also wanted to marry British and Puerto Rican marriage customs. I knew many of our friends had to leave their children behind, hire babysitters, and travel long distances, some from as far away as Asia, just to be with us, so the party had to be a nonstop affair full of surprises that blew them away. We also wanted our friends with kids to feel like they were on a second honeymoon, since kids weren't invited to the wedding.

The day of our wedding, I remember Nick and I looking around the reception room before any guests arrived. It was a pinch-me moment. There were Austrian crystal chandeliers, a lavish white carpet, rectangular white Lucite tables, die-cut embossed name cards with handwritten calligraphy, personalized menus, and vivid purple orchids flown in from Thailand. There was a seamless white dance floor with our wedding monogram in the center and a stage for the seven-piece band. To the side of the dance floor was a white lounge area with designer couches and mirrored tables boasting bottles of champagne in silver buckets. Purple was our accent color and also Nick's favorite color, and from then on would represent us as a couple. I had done everything in my power to make the event special, and my hard work had paid off.

When it was time for the day to begin, Nick and I were able to let go and have fun. Our family and friends couldn't believe how calm and collected I was, but all I could think was *Let the Cristal champagne flow. Now it is up to the universe and God to help make this an amazing day.*

Our guests arrived, dressed to impress and celebrate, with men in dashing tuxedos and women in long black dresses styled with fancy fascinators, just as I had imagined. I had seen the weather forecast three days earlier and knew it would be on the chillier side in the evening, so I made sure that every woman had a black pashmina handed to her when she arrived at the ceremony. My wish was for our guests to feel glamorous while also being able to comfortably enjoy the evening.

When Nick walked to the altar to take his place, clad in a custom-made midnight-blue Tom Ford tuxedo, the same style that Daniel Craig wore as James Bond in *Skyfall*, you could hear a pin drop. The cue for our wedding procession to begin was none other than a live instrumental version of the *Goldfinger* theme song. My nephew and niece were the last of the wedding party to walk down the aisle—the handsome ring bearer followed by the adorable rosy-cheeked flower girl. Next, two male friends with white gloves carried a white and purple-trimmed regal banner in Swarovski crystal that read *Here Comes the Bride . . .* And then it was my turn.

As soon as I heard the first live notes of Edith Piaf's "Hymne à l'amour," I took a very deep breath, said a quick prayer with the sign of the cross, and latched arms with Tío Rafael. I reminded him to walk slowly and take it all in, and positioned my *Vanda* "blue magic" orchid bouquet at my waist for my walk down the aisle. With the nearly finished Freedom Tower and Gothic, Romanesque, and Art Deco Tribeca buildings as my backdrop, I took each step with deliberate grace and appreciation for everyone and everything around me. My long brown hair flowed around my shoulders, accented by a six-foot white veil, incorporating part of my Mami's wedding gown, that trailed behind me.

I won't even pretend to be modest here: *I felt stunningly gorgeous.* I was beaming and glowing.

By the time I reached the end of the aisle, I was overcome with a kind of happiness I had rarely known before or since. Seeing the empty chair to the right of the altar with a silken purple ribbon around the backrest securing a card that read *In loving memory of the late Edwin Arroyo Mora, father of the bride* brought tears to my eyes. I had designed that detail in honor of my father's physical absence and his spiritual presence. However, I had no doubt that he was there with me that day in spirit, right next to me at the altar.

I glanced over to my beloved *tío* Rafael. It was always his dream to give me away. When at long last I took my last few steps to stand at Nick's side, a sense of peace like I had never known washed over me. I was forty years old, marrying my very own James Bond, surrounded by everyone dear to us in a unique ceremony that is forever etched in my mind. As the sun set behind us on the Hudson, I will never forget how the crystals hanging from the clear Lucite wedding gazebo created their own music as the wind gently blew. Dusk turned into night, and we exchanged personalized vows, sealed the ceremony with the kiss of all kisses, and listened to "The Impossible Dream" being sung a capella in the background as we walked back up the aisle, hand in hand, with wide smiles as the new Mr. and Mrs. Farley. Of course, we were eager to pop a bottle of Cristal 2005 to start the official celebration.

Unbeknownst to me, while I rejoiced in the union with my soul mate, a thunderstorm was brewing inside my body. The health diagnosis that would change my life forever was not a million miles away, but despite all the cues from my father's spirit, my spot-on inner voice, and the universe at large, I didn't have a premonition at that moment in time. On the happiest day of my life, everything was right in the world.

9

In Sickness and in Health

Realize deeply that the present moment
is all you ever have.
—ECKHART TOLLE

Our fairy-tale nuptials went off without a hitch, and the figurative icing on our divine wedding cake was a spectacular sixteen-day honeymoon in Bora Bora. We chose this spot because neither of us had ever been there, we had included it on our life list, and it seemed the perfect place to decompress after a year of wedding duties. To say we were ready to embrace the serenity of French Polynesia is an understatement.

So we jetted off on May 19, and twenty-four hours later made ourselves at home in a slice of heaven nestled in the most striking lagoon I have ever seen. Our overwater villa at the St. Regis had a 24/7 butler and a private outdoor pool facing the famous Mount Otemanu, and was our home for the next two weeks. We ate at the Lagoon Restaurant by Jean-Georges, lazed around on our villa deck, took walks through the lush grounds of the hotel, and reveled in having so much time together, alone at last.

We were all set to live it up on our honeymoon—and knock a few items off our life list while we were at it. Scuba diving was on the list, and since Nick was a certified diver, I let him lead the way. I loved floating on the surface of the crystal clear waters with my hunk, in awe of the varied marine life below. But when it was time to go underwater, I was terrified. I found it hard to control my breathing, trust my equipment, and believe I wasn't going to end up in a watery grave. Nick held my hand and after a few attempts I was able to overcome my fear. We descended a few meters and I was suddenly surrounded by the fish I could see from the surface. It was an incredible feeling to float weightlessly, just the sound of my bubbles streaming past my mask, observing my fishy friends. I walked away feeling like there was no greater beauty and mystery than what is found in the great waters beneath us.

That evening Nick had a romantic surprise for me. All he told me was that a boat would pick us up at 5:15 p.m. and to dress to the nines. As we approached the main entrance docking area, we were directed to a boat, where a captain welcomed us. As it turned out he wasn't just the captain but a bartender who made killer mai tais and strummed a ukulele. Talk about a jack-of-all-trades!

Once aboard, we sailed down the lagoon to our secret destination: a private island where we would spend the evening together. There I noticed a platform on the beach, literally over the water, that held a table for two under the stars. And guess what? Our captain was also a chef! He prepared a five-course dinner with dishes that would not be out of place in a Michelin-starred restaurant. And as the plates were cleared away, he emerged from the kitchen carrying four lighted sticks and proceeded to juggle fire for entertainment! I honestly felt like we were on *The Bachelor* and Chris Harrison was going to pop out at any second! Nick always sets a high bar for himself, but this one would be hard to top!

Next I felt it was my turn to do something special for my new husband. The day before we were scheduled to fly back home, our last dinner was at the Lagoon by Jean-Georges terrace. I arranged for the hotel general manager and staff to help me orchestrate a fireworks show over the lagoon. At the end of the display I had them bring out a bottle of 1982 Château Pichon Longueville Comtesse de Lalande, a sensual, elegant, and historic vintage, one of our favorite Bordeaux wines, with a note saying, "I love you forever, Mr. Bond." I will always remember the way he turned and looked at me when he realized the fireworks were for us and the way his face lit up when he saw the Lalande. This was the pinnacle of our honeymoon. We were such a perfect match. We were meant for each other. We had found our soul mates.

Suffice it to say that our honeymoon was out of this world and I could not help but cry when it was time to go home. While at the hotel, we created a heartfelt bond with the hotel staff who had looked after us during our stay—from the butler who organized anything our hearts desired to the sommelier at the Lagoon by Jean-Georges who introduced us to incredible wines and champagnes. They made our time very special and became like friends to us. I think we also made a lasting impression on them!

Once home in New York City, I was eager to start our lives as newlyweds. Just after we got back, we closed on our first apartment together and scheduled a few trips to Europe in July and early September—the first for John's graduation and the second to celebrate my Mami's sixtieth birthday. In between, we would move into our new home after completing a few adjustments to the space—all incredibly exciting. We were sitting on top of the world, having the absolute time of our lives together.

Our blissful streak was to soon come to an abrupt pause. A few months after we returned from our honeymoon, my beloved *abuela* Esperanza died. Mami had come to New York a few weeks earlier to help us with the move into our apartment and see her mother before the three of us were to leave for Europe for an entire month. We would stay in one of Nick's two apartments in London, an old warehouse conversion in Bermondsey. Nick would work out of his London office and Mami and I would visit the sights in London before traveling to Paris and Florence. Although we didn't realize it at the time, my *abuela* was living out her last days in our world and the end was near for her. One morning after she had eaten breakfast, Esperanza passed away peacefully in her sleep. There was no illness or disease; it was simply old age. Esperanza had lived ninety-five amazing years. We should all be so lucky.

Mami and I immediately left for the Bronx, where I helped Tío Rafael with funeral arrangements and booked tickets for my entire family to fly to Puerto Rico to lay Esperanza to rest. The timing of Mami's birthday trip to Europe was not ideal, but I saw it as a blessing in disguise during a time when she had to say a sorrowful goodbye. Abuela Esperanza wouldn't have wanted us to cancel this trip on her account.

When we returned stateside, Mami flew back to her home in California, and Nick and I got to furnish our apartment. We wanted to transform it into our dream oasis in the city. The space was much larger than the apartment we had lived in when we first got together, so we bought new furniture and art. It was an opportunity for me to imprint my personality on our home. I married bursts of color with the monochrome bachelor-pad styling Nick had brought with him. Luckily, we both have the same taste in décor and style, so there were no disagreements about what to buy. The result: a happy, modern, contemporary, and welcoming home.

A few months before our wedding, Nick and I began discussing our options for permanent contraception; in fact, the topic came up on our first date when Nick gently asked, "Are you open to not having children?" I now know that this was his British way of saying, "I really don't want any more kids." Not even entertaining the possibility of having children had been a deal breaker with Romeo, but Nick let me know he wasn't ruling the possibility out. Four years on and my desire to be a mother had changed. I knew that carrying and delivering a healthy child would be hard for me, given the shape of my uterus and ongoing fibroid issues. It didn't seem right to put my and my unborn child's life at risk with such a pregnancy.

I had spent my entire life wanting to keep the option open to have children, but until now I had never stopped to consider if this was what *I* really wanted. Yes, I loved children and would have loved to be a mom. But was it something I had to do at all costs? Was I willing to risk my health or lose the love of my life over this? Certainly not. I had reached a point where it was no longer a priority. After meeting Nick, I realized that a life of adventure and adoration with my partner in crime was all I needed. Plus, I am head over heels in love with my role as an aunt to my awesome niece and nephew, whom I can gush over, spoil rotten, share my life lessons with, and introduce to everything the world has to offer. Some may call our decision selfish or think I am missing out or feel I will never be complete without experiencing the joys of my own child, but I don't agree. A woman shouldn't have children because she is biologically expected to; she should have them because she wants them more than anything in the world.

Let's be honest here. I abso-freakin'-lutely love my life. I value my husband and the freedom we have to hop on a plane and travel to faraway lands on a whim. We can stay up until the small hours of morning and wake up at noon if we want. We have the time and disposable income to throw fabulous parties, help others in need, give back, and fulfill our roles as husband and wife as we see fit. And as I would soon learn, as health issues became increasingly front and center in my life, more so than worrying about not being able to give our children lives they deserve, we can devote our time to caring for others and each other, and that is more than enough for me.

Nick considered a vasectomy but we decided against it because of concerns about its effectiveness. I would be the 1 percent minority that gets pregnant after the man has the surgery! The onus was on me. When I discussed options with my ob-gyn, she initially suggested an IUD, but—given my track record with rare medical conditions—I could only imagine how that might affect my body, causing some new and complex repercussion. My gut also told me an IUD wasn't for me. Then she mentioned another option, called Essure. This consisted of two coils surgically inserted in the fallopian tubes to block them and prevent fertilization. The option was less drastic than tying my tubes but effective, so we decided to go ahead with it.

I had the procedure two months prior to our wedding, but when I awoke, I was told they had difficulty placing the coil in the right tube and had only managed to get the left one done. My doctor suggested we give it another shot, which we did two weeks later, but it was unsuccessful. Not only that, it seemed the left coil was no longer in place, which led them to believe I had passed it without noticing.

Something clearly wasn't quite right down there, and during my yearly checkup we got to the bottom of my issues. In the months leading up to my checkup, I had been suffering bouts of irregular bleeding, spotting between periods, cramps, and sharp pain during intercourse, but the most alarming of all was the heavy bleeding and huge clots I flushed down the toilet once a month during my period. It was so bad that I had to double up and use both tampons and pads, and still changed them every couple of hours or so before they were soaked through. The IBS panic attacks had returned, now triggered by my monthly cycle. I was in constant pain. Our lives were suddenly turned upside down by the issues I was having. All I wanted was for things to go back to normal. On top of it, I had lost a lot of weight, my belly was protruding, and I felt tired all the time. I had a sense that something was wrong. My body was clearly trying to tell me something, and I wanted to get to the bottom of it once and for all. I had had enough.

My ob-gyn, Dr. Watts, immediately ordered a slew of exams and a routine ultrasound. As she reviewed the results, she sounded surprised when she said, "Wow, you have quite a lot of fibroids."

I had known about the fibroids since 1997; so had Dr. Watts. We had always made sure to monitor them, but it seemed they had grown aggressively since my last checkup.

Dr. Watts never truly communicated the gravity of fibroids to me; she never gave it to me straight, and since I was still green when it came to dealing with doctors, I failed to read her report and ask the right questions. You have to remember, growing up in Puerto Rico, doctors were like parent figures whom you didn't question: you took what they said and simply followed their advice and instructions. From what the doctor explained, I understood that I had more fibroids than expected, but I didn't find out how many or how large they really were until much later. I never asked for or reviewed her written report—lesson learned!

At the end of our appointment, Dr. Watts said, "I suggest you make an appointment with a surgeon to talk about your options, but I think you might need to consider a hysterectomy."

What? A hysterectomy? I had come to this appointment hoping to understand what was going on with me and maybe consider a pill to make things better—not to hear it was time to get rid of my entire reproductive system. As I left the doctor's office to consider her suggestion, a silver lining came to mind. A hysterectomy would take care of the contraception issue. It would also decrease my odds of getting ovarian cancer.

A few days later Nick and I met with my surgeon, Dr. Veronica Lerner from New York University (NYU) Medical Center, who recommended a total hysterectomy, which would involve removing my uterus, fallopian tubes, and cervix but would keep my ovaries intact. I knew not removing my ovaries would leave me open to the risk of ovarian cancer. I insisted that Dr. Lerner remove them, too, but she advised against it, because it could send me straight into early menopause. Nick also insisted that I keep them, as they protect you not only from early menopause but also from heart disease and osteoporosis. I went against my gut feeling, listened to them instead, and to this day I regret that decision. Within four months of my hysterectomy, I was hit with early menopause anyway, complete with major hot flashes. And I still have a fear of ovarian cancer on top of it all.

I regretted not listening to my guiding voice. Everything health-wise with me had to be complex, cumbersome, stressful. The menopause symptoms were particularly unpleasant; the terrible hot flashes were as if someone had lit me up on fire. At night my bed was drenched with sweat; I felt weak, tired, mentally exhausted. What also worried me was how my sex drive, my libido, would be affected. I understood the importance of intimacy, sex, connecting with your partner, and here was yet another roadblock.

I honestly never stopped to think about the meaning and emotional consequences of having a hysterectomy. As so many women do, I simply followed the doctor's advice and didn't question it. At the time it felt right and logical, but I wasn't at all prepared for the aftermath.

The other part of my body that was concerning me during this period were my breasts. I had noticed a change in them a few months earlier; something felt off with my breast implants. I originally had silicone breast implants back in 2003 when I turned thirty in an attempt to compete with the stick-thin, big-breasted blond women of Orange County. Those implants had been replaced in 2011 with saline implants that better suited my figure by a renowned Park Avenue plastic surgeon. But now, not only did they feel like they were deflated, I had the sense that they were leaking. So, in early 2014, around the same time as I was considering the hysterectomy, I decided I should have my breast implants looked at.

I wanted concrete and permanent solutions that would stabilize my health and allow me to take control from whatever was causing harm inside my body. If that meant having to press "pause" on my life to get these surgeries out of the way, so be it.

When it came to my breast implants, I saw a fantastic breast reconstruction surgeon with breast cancer experience named Dr. Sayer. I fell in love with her the instant I met her, and she is my doctor and friend to this day. She was thorough with her explanations, giving me several options, and together we came up with a plan that best fit my needs. That appointment was my first lesson on how I should expect to be treated as a patient. Ever since, I haven't expected anything less.

Dr. Sayer explained that I was probably having an allergic reaction to the saline implants and recommended I remove them completely. She also said that she would advise not replacing them with silicone implants immediately. My breast cavities needed time to heal. This would mean I would be flat-chested until I could have the reconstruction surgery, which could be a year away. I couldn't quite bring myself to accept such a measure, especially since I was a young newlywed with so much more to look forward to on an intimate level with my husband. I knew it would have an impact on our love life, so I opted for immediate reconstruction with silicone "gummy bear" implant replacements.

I was set to rearrange my female anatomy, all in one fell swoop. Due to the doctors' schedules, I began with the breast reconstruction, followed by the hysterectomy ten days later. The doctors belonged to different medical institutions and both warned me that going from one major surgery to the next in such a short period of time would not be easy to handle. Even so, my mind was made up. I knew how much strength I had, and I felt capable of withstanding any amount of hardship. All I wanted was to reclaim my life and move forward with my husband.

I needed to be in control. I felt like my health was out of control, a 747 without a functioning cockpit. There was also the pressure of being a newlywed. I felt a mixture of guilt and fear with regard to Nick. Guilt for bringing this chaos to our marriage. Fear that he'd walk away. I had barely had the chance to live life with Nick, as most new married couples envision. It was one curveball after another, and I couldn't help feeling like we were striking out with each pitch.

There was something else worrying me too. I have such sensitive pigmentation, every cut leaves a mark that takes forever to disappear. Dr. Sayer warned me that the breast reconstruction surgery would involve making incisions. The idea of yet more scars made me extremely uncomfortable. My body was about to dramatically change not just from the inside but also the outside. Would Nick see me differently? It was scary, but I couldn't dwell on it too much or I'd back out.

With my breast reconstructive surgery set for the end of May and my hysterectomy scheduled for June 10, Nick and I decided to celebrate our first wedding anniversary resting and relaxing in St. Bart's. As we flew into the tiny airport of St. Bart's, the light aircraft skimming over the mountaintop before swooping down to the runway below, I wondered if the precariousness of the landing and the wondrous views of the island on arrival were somehow a sign of what was to happen over the next few weeks. Two major surgeries but afterward a period of stability and a chance to really enjoy my new married life with Nick.

The breast reconstruction surgery went incredibly well despite the fact that it took eight hours to complete. I was awestruck from the moment I woke up. Normally, surgical anesthesia always sends me into a post-op nightmare, but this time around it was like waking up from a long and deep sleep, with no violent nausea or vomiting. Nothing. The surgeon and anesthesiologist were angels sent straight from heaven. So much so, that I asked the latter for the drug combo recipe he had used, hoping to share it with the future hysterectomy anesthesiologist. It was like landing a golden ticket. Then, when I was able to catch a glimpse of my reconstructed breasts, I was shocked to see that they actually looked normal—in fact, better than normal; they were perfect. Something I desperately needed as I was about to go into a surgery that would strip me of my most vital feminine organs.

One surgery down, one to go. Maybe it was too much to expect my body to come through for me twice in a row. My hysterectomy went terribly. While being prepped in the pre-op room, the anesthesiologist came by for the routine preparation; and when I mentioned the breast reconstruction surgery days before and handed her a copy of the anesthesia report so she could duplicate the magic cocktail, she had a very uncaring response: "Well, I'm going to do it my way," which included an epidural. I was terrified, plus I knew from all my friends who had kids how much it hurt to have this done. Clearly this anesthesiologist lacked compassion for a patient expressing great concern, not to mention a frequent OR flyer! Although I was doubtful about her course of action, I had no choice, as I was already in the operating room. I prayed to God to keep me safe. I was in such a vulnerable state, right before surgery, with little reassurance that I would be okay. It's funny, but at that moment I felt like I was at the DMV: "Now serving number 152." I was treated like a number and not a woman undergoing invasive surgery.

I prayed to God, the angels, and the spiritual guides—all

those that I couldn't touch or see in the physical world but have always accompanied me—to keep me safe.

Although the surgery itself went well, what followed was extremely harrowing and distressing. Within the first few hours of recovering, with Nick by my side, I was overcome by intense head-to-toe shivering. I was pale and felt extremely weak. It was so severe that Nick yelled for help. When the nurse realized I had a fever of 107 degrees, she cleared the area and called for backup. I could hear a massive commotion in the distance, then a group of doctors surrounding my gurney.

I still don't know exactly what happened or what caused my body to react in such a sudden and aggressive manner. I was kept under observation in recovery for nine hours before they took me to a semi-private room. I then began to vomit violently. If only that anesthesiologist had followed my suggestion!

Twenty-four hours later I continued to vomit. But my biggest concern was that I could not feel my legs. The epidural had numbed me from the waist down, but forty-eight hours later no movement had returned. Thoughts of permanent paralysis crossed my mind as I pushed my brain to send a signal to my feet to wiggle my toes and nothing happened. *Is this it? Will I be paralyzed for life now?* I felt momentarily what people must feel when they wake up from an accident and can't feel their extremities. The first shift nurse kept reassuring me this was normal, but I didn't believe her. I knew plenty of people who have had epidurals and they recovered feeling in their legs within hours. Was there a surgical complication? What were the doctors hiding from me?

In a panic, I called Dr. Sayer and told her what was happening.

"Zulema, that is not normal. This could mean permanent

damage. Your surgeon, Dr. Lerner, needs to see you immediately to assess the situation."

I hung up and buzzed for the nurse. "I want your supervisor, and I want your supervisor's boss right now," I demanded angrily.

When the doctor on call entered the room and examined me, he confirmed my suspicions and Dr. Sayer's assessment: movement should have returned to my legs after a certain number of *hours*, not days! The nurses on call should have reported it immediately.

This episode later helped me deal with an anesthesiologist at MD Anderson Cancer Center who refused to answer my pre-op questions and disregarded my concerns. I stopped the surgery and respectfully demanded a new anesthesiologist. I felt terrible backing up the OR, but after this horrible incident at NYU Langone Medical Center, I wasn't about to be put under anesthesia by someone who made me feel uncomfortable. An anesthesiologist's job is to address your concerns in a compassionate, caring way. At the end of the day, you are a client paying for a service. You have every right to ask for a different anesthesiologist to provide you the service you expect.

I had been through my share of post-op recoveries, but the NYU hysterectomy took the gold medal. I still cringe thinking about it now. I hated every moment of my experience at NYU. There were no private rooms available; my fellow patient in the room cried and yelled all night from pain. I felt terrible for her because her nurses and team were not able to manage her pain. I couldn't rest.

By the time NYU released me, I had set up two nurses on twelve-hour shifts for at-home care for the next two weeks. I had been told such a surgery could potentially lead to excessive bleeding and excruciating pain and discomfort. Nick was willing to do anything for me, but I did not want Mr. Bond to carry the burden of such intense care. Plus, it was such an intimate part of my body—one that I hoped he would continue to find sexy—so I wanted to shield him from something so personal and private.

The nurses left two weeks later. Exhaustion combined with a deep emotional toll set in. I had been on Vicodin around the clock to alleviate waves of searing pain and was left with no energy to deal with the depression that pummeled me like a tsunami. It was very different from the depression I suffered during my sexual harassment and as a result of the financial crisis. No one on my team of doctors—not even Dr. Lerner, who does this procedure regularly—nor any of my friends warned me that, regardless of how psychologically prepared you might think you are, a hysterectomy wreaks havoc on your emotions and body. And, frankly, the doctors acted like it was as simple as pulling a tooth. Had this been the right option for me? Had I been selfish? Would I regret this later?

Anger overpowered any type of logic or reasoning at that point. I was angry at my body because it had let me down so much. I was angry at Dr. Lerner. I was angry at NYU and the anesthesiologist. Of course I knew there were fibroids—some of which I later found out were the size of grapefruits!—that had to be removed. Of course I understood that a hysterectomy was my best bet. But when my mind ran wild, none of that mattered anymore. Self-pity kicked in. I felt as if I were drowning and there was no amount of love, care, or affection that could rescue me from this black hormonal hole. My healing process was slow. It was unbearably *lonely*. No one ever asked me, "How are you doing emotionally?" Many of my friends acted as if it were just another surgery—a sign of ignorance, because women don't talk about the emotional toll of a hysterectomy. And yet it's one of the most common surgeries among women in the United States.

Nick never left my side. He assured me over and over that losing my "womanhood" didn't affect my gorgeousness. In the end, however, he couldn't understand the depths of what I was experiencing. I didn't expect him to. Furthermore, I don't think I was even able to communicate it clearly, because I didn't quite understand it myself. I was lost and all I felt was an emptiness— like my womanhood had been mutilated, like my organs had been ripped out of my body, leaving me barren. I felt a tremendous and unexpected sense of loss and grief. I felt as if I had lost a child. I know now that I was grieving the loss of my reproductive system. Worse still, I didn't feel better for having had the surgery; I felt worse. My mind was restless too. There were many nights I went to bed crying. My womb had betrayed me, my reproductive system had betrayed me, and NYU Langone Medical Center had betrayed me too. I was a mess.

I knew it wasn't okay to feel this way, but I didn't want to admit it to anyone because I felt like no one would understand. After all, it had been my decision to have the surgery, so the consequences were my responsibility. I put on a brave face in public, but inside I was shattered. I knew I needed a change of scenery. Continuing to stay at home lying in bed would drive me out of my mind. So, six weeks after the surgery, Nick took two weeks of vacation and we left for the South of France. Travel is often my salvation, and yet again it rescued me. The time we spent in Cannes, Saint-Tropez, and Monaco reassured me I was still a woman, even without my reproductive system.

My agony and anguish slowly started to subside. I became more accepting of my new body, yet the medical advice of no baths, no pools, no saunas, no hot tubs, no beach, and absolutely no sex for three months was a hard reminder that things were not yet normal for me. My breasts were gradually healing, too, so any sort of intimacy for Nick and me was a true challenge during that period in our relationship. Boy, it was hard. At times I felt that he was withdrawn, which threw me into fits of worry. I didn't want anything to change between us. I was already worried that our intimacy might suffer after the hysterectomy—and now it seemed it *was* suffering. Here we were, at the dawn of our second year of marriage, and I feared that I couldn't satisfy Nick as his wife. I knew his love for me was stronger than anything else, but sex has always been a very important part of our relationship, and I wanted him to feel loved and cared for the way he loved and cared for me.

As if that weren't enough on my plate, I also had to deal with invasive and inconsiderate questions about having children that were fired at me incessantly like blazing bullets. Blame it on my age or the fact that I was married and childless, but strangers—anyone, frankly—felt like they had the right to ask me about one of the most personal decisions one can make.

"Do you have kids?" they'd ask while I was waiting in line at the supermarket or sitting in the waiting room of my doctor's office.

"No," I would respond calmly.

"Why not?" (Intrusive question number one.)

"Because I had a hysterectomy."

"Oh, but nowadays there are so many other ways you can have children."

Stop right there. You'd think the word *hysterectomy* would

shut the conversation down, but people think it's okay to pursue it further. Why? I'm not looking for your opinion, advice, or any of the other options available to me. Don't tell me I can adopt or have a surrogate or freeze my eggs at forty years old or fly to the freakin' moon and find my little miracle there. You don't know me, you don't know my story, and I am not inviting you to participate. So stop pushing. Just drop it.

Motherhood, for me, is a very personal subject, and with time I have learned how to handle these questions and conversations. But during my recovery, when I was doubting my every decision, they were terribly hurtful and infuriating. Many are fighting a battle you know nothing about: Be kind.

Four months after my hysterectomy, as all these thoughts and emotions assaulted my psyche, my body persisted in rebelling against my well-being. It started earlier that year with a sharp pain in the back of my eye. Then I began to have occasional and sudden blurry episodes. One moment I was fine, and the next I could barely read the street sign in front of me. Anxiety struck in darkly lit spots like bars or certain restaurants at night because I couldn't see clearly and feared I might trip and hurt myself. In July 2014, when I went for my routine eye exam, my optometrist immediately noticed spots in my retina. These, along with my symptoms, prompted her to say, "You need to see a retina specialist right away. Those dark spots are maybe tumors, and we need to rule out eye cancer."

This was the first time I'd heard the C-word in my life. My heart dropped. Nick's too. Thanks to Dr. Sayer, I found someone who could see me that same week.

The retina specialist that Dr. Sayer referred me to said he would need to perform a fluorescein angiogram, which in layman's terms is like an MRI for the eye. In order to perform this exam, first he would dilate my eyes with drops by injecting a yellow contrast dye through one of my veins. Then he would take black-and-white photographs of my retinas and examine them. However, in the two seconds that it took for the dye to be visible in the blood vessels of my eye, I was ambushed by the most unexpected and humiliating side effect I had ever experienced in my life: sudden vomiting and defecation. Yes, I went from panicking about what the yellow dye might reveal to soiling myself in the doctor's office in front of the technician. As it turns out, the eye can directly trigger the vagus nerve, and mine clearly does not work as it should. It was so awful, I didn't know what to do. I froze! The technician guided me to the bathroom, where I threw my panties away and did the best I could to clean myself up.

When I stepped out of the restroom, the technician asked me back into the doctor's office to continue the exam. *Really?* Always the trouper, I held my head up high and walked back in. My eyes were numb from the drops they'd administered earlier, so the doctor grabbed some metal hand tools and started literally poking my eyeball with force. I couldn't feel any pain, but I could see *everything*. It was one of the most bizarre and distressing exams I have ever had, and I've had my fair share. I did my best to withstand the discomfort and utter embarrassment in order to get to the root of my eye issues, but it was all in vain. The torturous hour-long exam and the photographs of my retinas revealed absolutely nothing.

"I don't know what you have," the retina specialist said. "I'm sorry, but I can't help you."

How many times do I have to hear this in my lifetime? And with that, he handed me off to a rare eye disease researcher who focused on cases such as mine and warned me that it could take up to a year to get a formal diagnosis. What? Isn't science supposed to give you answers?

On the cab ride home, I couldn't get over my disgraceful bodily reaction. I was mortified. Acutely aware of the leftover stench that accompanied me, I felt frustrated, irritated, and livid at the thought of yet another undiagnosed issue that needed solving. Wasn't the hysterectomy and breast reconstruction enough? When I called to make the appointment with the eye researcher, October was the earliest he could see me. I had no choice but to bite my lip and wait. The ticking clock was painful for me, but it was something that I was already too familiar with.

I often reflect on the many incomprehensible symptoms plaguing my life—the IBS, potential eye tumors, the strange reaction to the yellow dye—and I wonder whether there is a way to discover that perhaps all these seemingly disparate symptoms were related. How did my doctors not catch them during my annual checkups? How did I not realize that everything was in one way or another pointing in the same direction? There is no use asking such questions now, but I do sometimes wish I had been able to see things more clearly.

At the final hysterectomy checkup with the NYU surgeon, Dr. Lerner, I was thrilled to get her pronouncement that everything was fine. She said I was healing well and the pathologies had come back all clear. I left her office, called Nick, and said: "All good. I'm done. I'm done with the breasts; I'm done with the hysterectomy. We can finally move on." I made sure that "moving on" included having sex. Nick was thrilled. The time had come to once again express our love for each other physically.

I was excited yet also absolutely terrified to have sex after this anatomy-changing surgery. It was like being a virgin all over again, fearing that it would hurt and worried that I might bleed—not to mention dreading a possible IBS flare-up. My heart was racing, partly from my anxiety and partly from the anticipation of reconnecting physically with my husband.

Let's just say I had nothing to worry about.

A couple of weeks after I recovered from my hysterectomy and was told I could have sexual relations again, menopause set in. This included dreadful night sweats and hot flashes that I had been told I could avoid by keeping my ovaries. Yes, that's right: early menopause had come ferociously banging on my door. It was somewhat of a rarity, given my type of hysterectomy, but I seem to be the queen of rarities when it comes to health issues.

∽

The autumn leaves were bursting with an array of oranges and reds when I finally walked into the eye researcher's office at Columbia University in early October, ready to submit myself to a five-hour examination process in hopes of finally finding out what the hell was wrong with my eyes. It was long, it was grueling, and by the end of it he said, "You aren't going blind: you have photosensitivity." Big sigh of relief. I could handle issues with light—no problem. "But"—there is always a *but* in my diagnoses—"it's too early to tell if you have cancer of the eye. I need to wait a year, reexamine you thoroughly, and then compare the results. And hopefully by then I will be able to give you a diagnosis." In the meantime, he said, all I could do was breathe and be patient and take the necessary precautions to avoid irritating my photosensitive eyes. This was not what I was hoping to hear, but I had to live with it.

Given the range of symptoms I had been experiencing over the past several months, I wasn't too worried about having cancer. Eye cancer? Come on.

Besides, Nick and I were long overdue for our next adventure, and so that fall found us making a pit stop in London to meet up with Nick's sons and friends and then boarding a Virgin Atlantic Upper Class flight to Dubai, to cross off our life list the goals of visiting the Burj Khalifa, the tallest tower in the world, and riding a camel in the Arabian Desert like Lawrence of Arabia. I never even knew one could sandboard! It was surreal. Then we visited Abu Dhabi to check off two more items from our list: riding the fastest roller coaster in the world at Ferrari World and attending a Formula 1 Grand Prix together (the final F1 race of the year).

As long as we could help it, nothing would get in the way of our adventurous spirits and absolute desire to fulfill the list of dream trips and experiences we had put together on our third date. I was determined to continue living my life and doing what I loved with my husband. It was one of the only things that inspired me to push through the dark thoughts that would have otherwise taken over my mind. Exploring the world with Nick and doing what we loved wasn't just a way of escaping reality; it was my way of affirming my life.

However, while in London, after going to the bathroom, I got up and turned to flush the toilet. I was speechless and disgusted by what I saw. Bright red blood had splashed all over the toilet bowl. *What the hell is happening?* I asked myself. *I thought I was done with these medical nightmares.* I didn't know which opening the blood was coming from, so I told Nick to please take me immediately to the urgent care facility near the hotel. After an examination, the doctor said the bleeding was from my rectum and urged me to see my primary care physician when I returned home, as he was unable to clearly diagnose what was happening. I followed his orders but chalked it all up to the hysterectomy. I had read that it took a year or longer to heal from such invasive surgery, but I found it strange to be bleeding from the rectum and not the vagina.

Our original plan was to fly back to London together. Nick had to attend a week of meetings in London before we headed home, but on December 1, somber news changed those plans. Tío Rafael's life partner of thirty-two years, Mr. Jones, who had been like an uncle to me, passed away from Parkinson's disease. Mr. Jones and I shared a passion for Shirley Bassey, Broadway, and music of all kinds. More importantly, he was the love of Tío Rafael's life. I knew Tío Rafael would be devastated. My uncle needed me. I dropped everything, Nick flew to London, and I flew straight from Dubai to New York to help with funeral arrangements and to be with my uncle.

By mid-December 2014, we were back on a plane to California to spend the holidays with my family. I was still dealing with intermittent bleeding and constant fatigue, which I blamed on travel and the grief of the loss of Mr. Jones. My symptoms were only getting worse. I now felt discomfort in my left gluteal area and was tortured by what seemed like a sudden electrical current of pain shooting down my left leg. The pain shot from my pelvic area down to my knee in bursts that I would describe as contractions. By the end of December I had devised a way of sitting only on my right side to avoid putting any type of pressure on my left butt cheek.

And then one morning in the shower, I felt it: a hard bump like a golf ball near my anus. *Holy crap!* It scared me, as I hadn't noticed it before. My heart raced, but I took a deep breath and calmed myself down. I immediately thought to myself, *Dr. Lerner must have missed a fibroid.* I tried to play it off as something that I could take care of when I returned home, thinking there would be a harmless explanation and it could be easily removed. I had no idea that I had just felt the intruder that would bring my life crashing to the floor and permanently alter my journey, my health, and my purpose in this world.

10

Cancer Strikes

We shall draw from the heart of suffering itself
the means of inspiration and survival.

—WINSTON CHURCHILL

A clearly visible and palpable bump was nestled just on the edge of my left butt cheek and my anus. What was it? What did this mean? Worry breached my racing thoughts. *Could it be* . . . I stopped myself short of saying the C-word; I didn't want it in my vocabulary. It couldn't be . . . I needed to see an ob-gyn.

As soon as we landed in New York in early January 2015, I made an appointment with a new ob-gyn, Dr. Rachel, recommended by a friend. I was not comfortable I was getting the care I wanted with Dr. Lerner or from Dr. Watts, the ob-gyn I had been seeing up until now. Dr. Rachel was also at NYU and therefore would save us some time, as she would have easy access to all of my medical records from the hysterectomy surgery.

I walked into a small, sterile, very modern, white-walled examination room with no décor, changed into a white-and-blue patient's gown, and was helped up on the examination table by the assistant, my blood pressure skyrocketing. The assistant looked apprehensive and I knew this was abnormal. When the doctor walked in, I got into position and there it was, clear as day. She did not even have to examine me to see the lump pushing out of my skin. How crazy was that? Not wanting to say more, she ordered an MRI immediately.

The MRI appointment was scheduled for two weeks out, so instead of waiting around with our minds focused on the impending test, Nick and I took off to South Beach for a long weekend to celebrate my forty-second birthday with friends, including one of my dearest friends of nearly twenty-three years, Lisa Quiroz. At five feet two inches, Lisa, a Harvard graduate, was a towering force: a Latina, half Puerto Rican, half Mexican, a traiiblazer, an advocate for women, children, education, and those less fortunate. A keen eye for talent, a visionary mentor, astute, and what Lisa said, we did.

When we returned on Wednesday, January 21, I went in for the MRI. As the minutes ticked by inside the whirring and thumping machine that would soon determine my fate, images of my custom-made off-white Monique Lhuillier lace wedding gown flashed before me in stark contrast to the white hospital gown I was wearing. At that moment the dress, the lavish wedding, the trips, my Chanel handbags, and all our material possessions didn't matter anymore.

I somehow knew I had reached a turning point; I was absolutely certain my life was about to change drastically. I sensed I was about to be challenged in ways I had not been before. And as I lay there on the bed of the MRI machine, noises all around me, I heard it loud and clear: Spirit telling me I was going to need all of my inner strength as the outlook on my health changed.

So far, my life seemed to be blessed by incredible highs and ravaged by petrifying lows. A great career in California, then harrowing sexual harassment that led to a nervous breakdown and IBS; an exciting move to the Big Apple, then losing it all and hitting rock bottom; meeting the man of my dreams, then being diagnosed with Hashimoto's disease and gastroparesis; marrying the love of my life, then undergoing breast reconstruction and a hysterectomy. What was next? Was this going to be the end of the line for me? I didn't know what to expect anymore. If anything, life was clearly trying to teach me one of its most valuable lessons: the importance of living in the present. All I knew was that I couldn't focus too much on what *might* happen in the future. I needed to focus on what I had before me right there and then.

During the scan, the MRI technician pulled me out of the tunnel and casually said, "When are you scheduled for your biopsy?" First red flag. *Biopsy? This is not good,* I thought. *Nick is going to go crazy; he won't believe it.* I changed out of my hospital gown and into my regular clothes. As I hailed a cab to head back home, I kept going over what the technician had said. My mind kept reaching for the word I did not want to truly acknowledge. A voice from my gut said, *Brace yourself. This is bad.*

"Please don't worry. It's probably nothing," Nick said time and time again, until I fell asleep in his arms that night.

Then came the first unnerving call from Dr. Rachel. "I'm not sure what type of tumor this is," she said. "It is outside of my area of expertise. I suggest you make an appointment with a colorectal expert." I wasn't alarmed. I had seen colorectal specialists before and had undergone rectal prolapse surgery. Maybe this new bump, this tumor, had something to do with that procedure. I hung up and called my friend Lisa and she suggested I see an ob-gyn oncologist first. She contacted one she knew, a doctor who had treated her breast cancer eight years earlier, and by the following Monday, January 26, at 6:30 p.m., I was sitting in Dr. Rogers's office explaining my situation and showing her my medical records, including the MRI performed prior to my hysterectomy, which Dr. Lerner had specifically requested. A puzzled look crossed Dr. Rogers's face as she glanced at my latest MRI report and compared it to the one from June 2014, four days before the hysterectomy.

"Wait a minute," she said. "This MRI in June 2014 took place four days before your hysterectomy, correct?"

I nodded.

"Your tumor was seen and reported then by the NYU Langone Medical Center radiologist after that MRI. They knew it was there. They didn't tell you?"

My heart dropped into the depths of my stomach. What? How could this be? Was it true? Had this tumor been growing inside of me for seven months? And did the doctors at NYU Langone Medical Center fail to alert me to it?

Immediately my friend Lisa said in her New York *Boricua* accent, "I can't believe this, Zulema! You were misdiagnosed."

I started shaking. I felt I was going to faint.

As questions pierced my brain, Dr. Rogers conducted an exam, felt the tumor, and then said, "I don't think this is a regular carcinoma; this is something else. This could be sarcoma."

I had never heard the word *sarcoma* before and I didn't know what it meant. I asked, "What is that?"

"Oh, it's just a very fleshy tumor," she replied.

I exhaled slowly. *She didn't say* cancer. That was all I could think. *She did not say* cancer. From her calm demeanor and matter-of-fact response, I automatically assumed this tumor she was referring to was likely benign—nothing to worry about.

"The best thing you can do now is to go see a colorectal oncologist at MSK," she added.

Ding, ding, ding—another red flag! *Oncologist*—that usually meant only one thing, and Memorial Sloan Kettering *Cancer* Center . . . well, the name says it all. My anxiety sky-rocketed, but rather than let my emotions get the best of me, I followed the suggested steps and held on for dear life to the one remaining fact: No one had actually said the word *cancer* yet.

Three days later, after making an appointment with a colorectal oncologist, I was sitting at home, filling out Memorial Sloan Kettering's patient registration information, when I got a call from their social services therapy department.

"I'm very sorry about your diagnosis. We're here to help you," the woman said. "Do you want to set up an appointment with one of our therapists to talk about it? We know you're just starting this process, and we offer these services to all registered Memorial Sloan Kettering patients." What was she talking about? What diagnosis and why did I need a therapist? I mumbled something about getting back to her and put the phone down.

Nothing was making sense to me. I couldn't tie the pieces together. No one sat with me and said, "Listen, this is what's happening, and these are the steps we are going to take with your case." There was no clear path, and no one was giving it to me straight. I didn't even know what I had yet and neither did my new colorectal oncologist.

"Unfortunately, I can't give you an answer just yet," he said at our first appointment on Friday, January 30. "I need to present your case to the Memorial Sloan Kettering tumor and disease board."

I stared back, perplexed, as if he were speaking to me in a foreign language, then took a breath and asked him for further explanation. After so many years of dealing with doctors, I was beginning to learn. Never be afraid to ask questions when something a doctor tells you sounds like gibberish. It is every patient's right to know what their medical team plans to do with your body and your health.

"The tumor and disease board consists of a group of oncologists from different departments—medical oncology, radiology—and oncologists representing different types of cancer. Every Monday they meet in the Memorial Sloan Kettering executive boardroom and use that time to bring up the cases that need more attention than others. Then, as a group, we decide the best way to handle each case," he explained, and then added, "So, I will call you later next week with the outcome of that meeting and how we feel we should proceed."

Two weeks of appointments, exams, referrals, and still no answer. I was climbing the walls with all sorts of images and outcomes filling my every waking hour. Stress and anxiety were slowly gnawing away any traces of hope that this could be anything but cancer. My sight was set on the Memorial Sloan Kettering tumor and disease board's conclusion, but the waiting game was only just beginning. My doctor explained that the board was unable to assess my case that Monday due to technical difficulties with PowerPoint—that was how they presented cases—so we would have to wait patiently for one more week before coming up with a possible action plan. Technical difficulties with PowerPoint. What is difficult about getting PowerPoint to work? Frustration . . . exasperation—no word can truly convey the turmoil that was seething inside me. Not having control over what was happening to my body was driving me insane. Every minute, day, and week that passed felt like an eternity—an eternity during which the tumor, that thing that nobody was ready to call "cancer," continued to cause more pain.

When at long last I received the call from the colorectal oncologist, there was finally a plan in place, although it was lacking the answers I desperately needed to hear. First off, they were not proposing to do a biopsy. The biopsy would be invasive and might result in bleeding due to the vascular nature of the tumor and possible infection from the biopsy needle. The tumor had to be removed as soon as possible. Once they had extracted the tumor and received the final pathology report, they would be able to tell me what the next steps would be. I pressed the doctor for more answers, to give me a hint as to what type of tumor they thought I had, but he would not budge. Frustrated, I gave in, thinking, *The sooner I can get this tumor out of my body and know what the hell it is, the better!*

The doctor said he would be able to operate on me the following Wednesday. He normally didn't operate on Wednesdays, but since his schedule the following week was full and then he was going out of the country for two weeks, he had asked for special permission to do the surgery on Wednesday. He didn't want me waiting until he was back to have the surgery. I would be undergoing my third surgery in less than a year, complete with another round of anesthesia—which, knowing me, would likely represent another round of post-op mayhem.

As I put down the phone, the reality of what I was facing hit me. What was bulging out of my left gluteal area, that ominous bump that had made its presence known to me only a month and a half earlier, was likely cancer. That's why they wanted to operate as soon as possible. In my mind all roads led to that word. Everything was happening so fast; I was being swept along by a fast and furious surge I couldn't fully control and grappling with the uncertainty and gravity of my situation. I wondered how those brave men and women fighting abroad for our safety must cope with the daily anxieties they endured, putting on body armor and arming themselves to face the uncertainty and dangers of the battleground. My battleground was a very different place with an unseen enemy, but I didn't feel like I was wearing any body armor and didn't know yet how to arm myself against this invader. I looked to my spirituality for support, but it wasn't immediately forthcoming. There was just an emptiness.

Every day was a struggle. Every hour. Every minute. Every second. Nick did his best to keep me positive, talking me off the ledge many times, explaining the possible implications of what the doctors had said and what options were available to me, but no matter how hopeful and encouraging he tried to be, my heart was heavy with impending doom. Meanwhile, I went into research mode, a tactic I would continuously resort to as my health issues intensified. I looked up the only concrete word I had registered in the cluster of appointments I had been through: *sarcoma*.

Sarcoma, according to Merriam-Webster's online dictionary, is "a malignant tumor arising in tissue (such as connective tissue, bone, cartilage, or striated muscle) of mesodermal origin." There was that word *malignant*—another red flag.

With my surgery date set and some newfound knowledge of a world I prayed would not be my new reality, I turned to

Nick and said, "I really want to see my niece and nephew before my surgery . . . just in case."

Just in case I didn't come out alive. Jam Jam and Marie meant more than the world to me. The joy they brought me couldn't have been greater if they had been my own children. It was unmeasurable love. I needed a temporary escape to avoid losing myself in worry. We could have nice meals and fun, and I could endlessly hug and kiss them. I needed their unconditional and innocent love and affection. My sister, my mom, and my nephew and niece met us for a quick weekend escape in Las Vegas during Valentine's Day weekend, and it was exactly what I needed. The children were clueless about what was going on, and we kept it that way. I reveled in their love and laughter and did everything in my power to ignore the cloud looming over my life.

On Saturday, February 14, Nick and I separated from the family for a while to check off yet another life list item: a private helicopter tour of the Grand Canyon. One minute I was anxious and somber about my current state of affairs, and the next I was whisked away, flying high in the sky with Mr. Bond. Awestruck by the absolute beauty of one of the seven natural wonders of the world, it was easy to put my gloomy thoughts away for a while: the red rocks of the Grand Canyon seemed so peaceful and beautiful that surely nothing bad was going to happen.

Living in the present is what I try to do when times are challenging, but with a pending diagnosis that could change my life, I began to savor every minute as if it were my last. As we hovered over the Grand Canyon, I vowed to never take anything for granted, to live in the present not the future, to do the things I loved, to fully embrace the now, to learn to forgive and accept unconditional love. We only have one life to live, and it is up to us to make it fabulous, fulfilling, and unforgettable.

Reinvigorated by the weekend's cascade of joy and affection, I returned home to face whatever fate had in store for me.

First off, I contacted the nurses who had helped me after my hysterectomy to make sure they were available to care for me. My mom was flying in from California for the surgery, but I figured we might need all the help we could get. I had not been prepared for the hysterectomy. This time I prepared for the worst.

Then came the pre-op exams, along with the final meeting with the surgical oncologist, two days prior to the operation. Nick and I sat in his office and asked him to carefully walk us through the surgery. I needed to understand every detail of what was about to happen to my body. To be sure nothing escaped me, I even asked him to please use the colorectal and pelvic anatomy model on his desk to explain the procedure.

I cannot stress this enough: if you ever find yourself in a situation like this, ask questions and more questions. Do your homework in advance. Don't fear your doctor, as if he or she is God. Doctors are human, just like you. They should be capable of addressing all your concerns or pointing you in the direction of the answer if they do not have it. Why do I say this? Because that day, as I pushed to know more about the surgeon's plan, I discovered not only that my tumor was on the edge of my anal muscle but that it extended into my left gluteal muscle.

"What does this mean?" I asked, perplexed.

"That I won't know exactly how much of your anal and gluteal muscle I will need to remove until I'm in the OR," he said.

"How might this affect me?" I pressed.

"There's a possibility that you could wake up missing part of your rectum and gluteal area," he replied.

WTF? Did I hear right? My ears were ringing. Two days before the surgery, and he was telling me this now? I was furious. Why wasn't I told this before?

"Where is the plastic surgeon in all of this?" I asked. And to my astonishment there was no plastic surgeon on call for my procedure. As I stared at the doctor in consternation, he asked if I would like one to be there, and I replied without hesitation and somewhat irately, "Of course." What I really wanted to say was, "Are you freaking kidding me? You're telling me that I may lose part of my rectum and ass and there will be no plastic surgeon to assess and fix the damage caused by this extraction?" I was baffled. Flabbergasted. Furious. At this point it hit me that I had to take charge of the appointment.

"What about recovery?" I asked.

As it turned out, I would have yet another difficult road ahead of me. My bowel movements had to be as soft as possible, because any type of pressure in that area after surgery would be excruciating. I would not be allowed to sit down under any circumstances for the next six weeks. All I could do was stand or lie down; that was it. It was not an easy prognosis, but—having been through my fair share of complicated post-op recoveries—I knew I would be able to do what was required of me.

The next day I was in the plastic surgeon's office.

Thankfully, she was compassionate and understanding and did her best to put my mind at ease, but nothing at that point really could. I walked out of the building overwhelmed by all the details running through my mind. As a distraction, Nick suggested we go shopping in SoHo and then for lunch at Jean-Georges at the Mercer Kitchen. It was snowing—an actual snowstorm. We stepped off the E train at Spring Street and, arm in arm, navigated the drifts of snow that were fast piling up on the sidewalks and roads. And we went shopping. I don't remember for what, but it was a much-needed distraction and holding on to Nick as we crossed the streets, I felt safe and secure. He was my rock. I felt incredibly grateful to have such an amazing man by my side every step of the way while my anxiety levels went through the roof.

The day before my surgery, I was so tense that I could barely move my neck and shoulders. I had a permanent headache I could not shake. I decided to treat myself to a mani-pedi—with clear nail polish, since my nail beds had to be visible during the operation—and a massage, since it would be two months before I could have one again. However, I had to have my phone handy, as I was expecting calls from the MSK team to firm up details for the following day.

Lying facedown on the massage table with the masseuse working out the knots and kinks in my upper back, the phone rang. I quickly picked it up only to find a Cigna health insurance representative on the other side. "I have received all of your paperwork from Memorial Sloan Kettering, but before going further I want to say how very sorry I am that you have been diagnosed with cancer," she said. My heart stopped, my brain went blank, and all I could see projected on my mind's screen in big bold letters were the words *I have cancer*.

In all the doctor's appointments, exams, phone calls with specialists, nurses, technicians, you name it, not once had the actual word been used in conversation. I knew I had a tumor—yes, that word had become part of my new medical vocabulary—but no one ever said it was malignant; no one ever said it was cancer. Deep down, however, I knew it must be, since the surgery was at MSK, and they only see cancer patients. The representative continued, "I am part of a specific group that handles catastrophic cases," she continued. "I'm responsible for the *cancer* cases."

Cancer. Cancer. Cancer. Cancer. Cancer.

I felt like shouting back, "Nooooo, stop saying that word!"

As the woman continued speaking, I thought, *Why isn't my colorectal oncologist saying this to me? Why am I hearing that I have cancer through a health insurance representative hours before my surgery? Clearly she knows more than I do.*

Feeling extreme anxiety, I was overcome with self-doubt. Was I doing the right thing? Should I wait and find a team of doctors who would be more frank with me regarding my case before I had surgery? Questions flooded my mind as my massage came to an end, and I walked out of the salon in a daze.

I was now floundering in a sea of questions that hadn't been there before. I called Nick, sobbing hysterically as I made my way back home. When I reached our apartment, he was waiting with a very worried look on his face. We sat on the sofa and he held my hand, comforted me, and said, "What do you want to do? What do you need from me?" I said I needed to cry. He held me as I sobbed.

As thoughts galloped through my mind, I looked up at Nick and said, "I don't know what the future is going to hold, but I now know that I have cancer." He stared back at me in silence and disbelief. "Listen," I continued, "I don't know what's going to happen with the surgery tomorrow—if I'll come out of it or not—but if I do, we're going to need to seek out several opinions regarding my tumor." I wiped away my tears and went into my logical and practical mode, making lists of what would need to be done later, desperately attempting to fool myself into believing I had a handle on this situation, trying to wrap my head around what was likely to come. To this day, I regret not canceling the surgery at the last minute. I should have done so. I was still in the early days of learning how to be my own patient advocate. There were so many more questions, I needed to have asked and answers I needed to have received before submitting myself to the surgery. When I was later treated at the MD Anderson Cancer Center in Houston, I learned that my surgery would have been more effective if chemo had been used to try to shrink the tumor before surgery. But I was so frightened about this thing growing inside me and doing who knows what to my body, that all I wanted was to have it removed. My doctors were telling me to have the tumor removed as soon as possible—that definitely didn't sound good. I needed to act. But there was that inner voice again, this time telling me to question the decision to have the surgery. Up until then in my life I had always listened to my inner voice—it was rarely wrong. But in the turmoil of the moment and my panic to rid my body of the thing down there, I pushed it aside. I will always wonder how different my outcome would have been had I not proceeded with the surgery at MSK. Maybe I would not have had to live with the specter of positive margins, maybe the surgery would not have been so invasive.

The moment the nurse wheeled me out of the prep room to surgery was heart-wrenching. I cried uncontrollably as they took me away from Nick. I wondered if I would come out alive, but what I was most frightened of was waking up without my rectum or being told I had a late-stage cancer.

When I woke up from surgery, on February 25, 2015, I immediately locked eyes with Nick and asked, "Was it a spindle cell tumor?" I had done my research earlier and knew that a spindle cell tumor would likely be a sarcoma.

"Yes," he answered.

"Did I lose my rectum?"

"No," he replied.

That day is still a blur in my memory. Visiting hours were over at 8:00 p.m., and the only ones left at my bedside were those whom I had asked Nick to admit: Mami, Tío Rafael, and Lisa. Exhaustion drowned out all attempts by my mom and Tío Rafael to lighten the situation and make me laugh. Mami had not eaten anything since that morning, so they asked if it would be okay if everyone went to grab some food. I felt an overwhelming desire to rest, and although the pain was starting to kick in, I put my best face forward and urged them not to worry and go have dinner, assuring them I would be fine. But the truth of the matter was that I was very upset, terrified, and worried about my prognosis.

At about 9:30 p.m. the surgical colorectal oncologist came into my room, still wearing his surgical cap and scrubs, and asked me how I was holding up. We exchanged some small talk, and then I said, "I hear it's a spindle cell."

"Yes," he said. "It is most likely a sarcoma, but until we get the final pathology, I can't tell you which type or what stage. But I wouldn't worry about that now if I were you."

Dr. Rogers was the first to mention the word *sarcoma*, and it had been embedded in my brain ever since. That was why I could not believe my ears. *Really? You're telling me I have cancer, a very rare form at that, but I shouldn't worry about it?* I had no energy to react, but I sure wish I had been able to give him a piece of my mind. However, I did know that I had to obtain two other pathology opinions. This is the right course of action when you are diagnosed with cancer, particularly a rare type of cancer like sarcoma. The reason is that cancer institutions like Memorial Sloan Kettering Cancer Center, Dana-Farber Cancer Institute, and MD Anderson Cancer Center all have pathology experts that specialize in different types of cancer. Pathology opinions can vary, and you need to be certain of the type and stage of cancer you have. The only way to ensure this is to obtain three pathology opinions. Most insurances cover a second pathology opinion and a third if it's a preferred provider organization (PPO).

After the oncologist exited the room, the information he had just confirmed sunk in through my post-op stupor. Panic began to course through my veins. *Cancer. I have fucking cancer? Sarcoma. No idea what type or stage.* He also told me that he had left positive margins in my body to avoid compromising my rectum. This meant that the edges of the tissue removed in my surgery still contained some cancer cells, which was tremendously unnerving to hear. Having positive margins was like living with a ticking time bomb. Who knew when it might go off? Cancer. How could anyone rest or sleep after receiving such news?

It also made me angry with NYU Langone Medical Center. How could medical professionals be so careless as to not inform a patient of a tumor that turns out to be sarcoma? The hospital had put me at risk. This was the pivotal moment when I told myself that I would become a patients' advocate. My own patient advocate first, and then an advocate for others. This would be my way of dealing with the anguish, pain, suffering—and, more importantly, the anger.

At around one in the morning, my pain reached unbearable heights. I called the night nurse to administer Dilaudid.

Before leaving the room, he turned around and said, "I'm sorry. Do you mind if I ask you something?" I said I didn't mind. "You are so young, and you have this type of cancer . . . How did you find out? How did you notice the tumor?" I gave him the abridged version of what had happened over the course of the past few months. "I just can't believe it. You're one of the rare cases I have seen come in here with sarcoma at such a young age," he said. "Most people are in their sixties or seventies, and their sarcomas are in other parts of the rectum or pelvic area, but not in the gluteal and anal muscle like yours." In other words, mine was anal cancer, not rectal cancer. And there it was: someone else confirming it was sarcoma, someone else pointing out that this was indeed a rare case, and someone else who knew way before I did that the road ahead of me would be long and arduous.

As naïve as it sounds, I had always heard of rectal cancer, but I never knew one could get cancer of the anus. There is an incredible amount of stigma associated with anal cancer that doesn't attach to the others, and it's not just in Hispanic culture where talking about private parts is taboo. It is not a socially acceptable cancer. It is often wrongfully associated with sexual activity. I overheard someone once say I must have gotten it from having anal sex—in other words, accusing me of causing the cancer through my own actions. How ignorant! The fear of judgment leaves many anal cancer patients feeling isolated. I didn't want that for myself. I hoped my openness and honesty about the disease might save a life or help others heal. I feel anal cancer, whether carcinoma or sarcoma, is where colorectal cancer was before Katie Couric had a colonoscopy live on national television to build awareness and promote prevention or when men hid their testicular cancer because of embarrassment.

11

Hanging in the Balance
of Heartbreak and Hope

Raw naked grief, but all in sorrow, there is
always a flower of hope within reach. Dare to reach.
Don't let fear limit, don't let the past stop you.

—THERESE RASMUSSEN

On Thursday night, one day after my tumor surgery, my vision started to fail me. By Friday morning, February 27, the incoming text messages on my phone were deformed and blurry. I could not read the whiteboard in front of the bed either. I alerted my surgical colorectal oncology resident on call and said, "I can't read. I can't type. I feel dizzy and off," but was told it was likely from the stress of the surgery and coming to terms with the fact that I had cancer. My vision slowly returned over the next few hours and I refocused on my more immediate situation, but, like everything my body does, this was an early warning of further challenges that I would encounter down my medical road.

The oncology resident decided to discharge me that very afternoon, just two days after my surgery. I didn't feel I was ready to leave the hospital. I didn't feel right. My inner voice told me all was not well. Medical insurance companies these days want you to spend the least amount of time possible in hospitals to save money. Doctors and hospitals are feeling the pressure. So I was discharged. When I got home, Nick helped me take a quick shower—my first in three days—and I went straight to bed. The next thing I remembered was waking up to my body shaking uncontrollably, as if I were having a seizure. My body jerked so hard that it rose from the bed. I freaked out. Suddenly the right side of my face and right arm felt numb. Terror-stricken, I cried out to Nick. Thank God he happened to be next door in his office. He rushed in immediately, fearing the worst. In the midst of this, my phone rang: it was Dr. Sayer calling to check up on me. She told Nick to take me back to the hospital immediately because she was worried I was having a seizure or a transient ischemic attack (TIA)—in other words, a mini-stroke.

Three hours after being discharged, I was back on a gurney at the Memorial Sloan Kettering emergency room, being pushed straight into an MRI of my brain. After the MRI, a myriad of other tests were conducted. In the end, no signs of stroke were evident, but they decided to keep me under observation that night, which meant having cables stuck to my head, ears, heart, fingers, legs, and feet to monitor my activity closely in case I had another episode. I was still on the gurney, because the ER was full. I was frightened and vulnerable, in a cold and clinical room, stripped of any comfort, feeling like some sort of Frankenstein-like scientific experiment.

When morning came, the results were still inconclusive, but I was stable, so they sent me home with an appointment to see the chief head-and-neck oncologist a couple of days later. After asking me a slew of questions, mostly about symptoms and what had happened, it was decided that I didn't have a

TIA or anything neurological. To this day I still don't know what happened to me that afternoon. Thankfully, it hasn't happened again.

The following week was absolute hell. The anal pain was agonizing, the nausea from the heavy painkillers truly crushing. And then it happened: the dreaded pangs alerting my brain that the time had come for my first post-surgery bowel movement. I had followed the doctor's orders to the letter, doing everything in my power to keep my stool soft by regularly taking Colace and magnesium, and now it was the moment of truth. As I walked to the bathroom, I was assailed by ripples of stress and anxiety. I felt weak; my legs wobbled. I was overcome by fear of pain. I carefully sat on the toilet seat, ready for my day of reckoning, tears streaming down my face, gasping for air. A barrage of yelling, sobbing, and screaming bloody murder quickly followed.

The pain was excruciating and the result was indeed straight out of a horror movie, with bright red blood splattered all over the toilet bowl. The doctor had warned me that this would happen and that it was normal, but nothing can prepare you for such a sight. It was terrifying and only the beginning.

Time steadily crawled by and my recovery was slow and painful. The crimson-tinted toilet bowl became a light pink, a sign that I was healing. Bone-weary and overwhelmed, I limited my visitors to only a few friends, but I found specific solace in one particular friend: Therese Rasmussen.

We had met back in 2006, at a mutual friend's wedding in Ecuador, and became fast friends. Breast cancer came knocking on her door back in 2013, but she seemed to have gotten the upper hand and by 2014 was told she was in remission. She spent the next six months celebrating this news, thinking that it would all be smooth sailing from that point onward.

Before my procedure, I told Therese that all the signs pointed to my having cancer. She confessed, to my great dismay, that her cancer had returned. It had spread and there was now nothing else they could do for her; it was only a matter of weeks before she succumbed to the illness. It made me feel guilty about my situation, but I could not help wondering if I would have the same outcome.

We continued to talk and text every single day. She understood my emotional turmoil right off the bat and was instrumental in helping me through those first few weeks while I grappled with the fact that I had cancer. I listened to her every day and tried to offer support as she went through weekly blood transfusions to help extend her life and time with her husband, Carl, and their two daughters. It was so difficult to hear the details of what she was going through as she reached the end of her life. Talking to her every day became one of the most important lifelines in my postsurgical recovery. It was my first time being so close to someone who only had weeks to live.

I talked to her about things I did not feel comfortable telling anyone else—my fears, my anxieties, my moments of sheer panic—and she was always there as an emotional rock. I had always figured those childhood friends with whom I had remained close would be my sounding boards, but that was not the case.

During one of our many phone calls, around early March, Therese shared a life-giving and selfless request. As she came to terms with the nearing of the end of her life, she realized there was so much more she would have liked to have done and accomplished, and she did not want her friends to have the same regrets. She asked all of her friends to stop what we were doing, write up our own life lists, and send them to her. Her wish was to make one of our life list items come true before she died to show us how important it was to not postpone our goals or our happiness.

Thrilled, her friends took up the challenge, but in return they challenged her to do the same. In recent years Therese had taken up photography and honed her skills to produce breathtaking images, so it was no surprise that having her own photograph exhibition was at the top of her list. When her friends saw this, they quickly got to work and managed to secure a gallery in Connecticut. Therese's first-ever exhibition was scheduled for Friday, March 20, in just two weeks, as time was obviously of the essence. Formal invitations were sent out while Therese focused on selecting images and writing captions for them with her daughters.

March 20 was less than a month after my surgery. I was still in full recovery mode and could not yet sit down, and after I developed flu-like symptoms days before the exhibition, my oncologist told me to stay away from crowds, as my immune system was working overtime to help me heal. As much as I wanted to be there for Therese, I didn't think I would be able to pull it off. I expressed my regrets, to which she replied, "Don't worry: I'm going to have a greenroom where I can rest, because it's going to be tiring for me to see all of those people, so you are welcome to use it with me."

Trying to let her down gently, I said I would try but could not promise to be there.

"For some reason I know you're going to be there, so I'm not worried," she said.

Her determination fueled my own. Deep down, I knew

it would likely be the last chance I would get to see her. Giving her a heartfelt hug in person and being there for her big debut suddenly became my driving force and goal. It felt good to focus on someone else for a change. After all the support Therese had given me over the past several months, I just knew I had to be there for her. Although Therese and I had been good friends for many years, the connection that we formed toward the end of her life was very different from the friendship we had previously shared. It was as if our souls had become intertwined; I felt her pain and she felt mine. And when she finally lost her battle with cancer and departed this life, I could still feel that connection.

As Friday approached, we hit an unexpected roadblock: there was a massive snowstorm angling straight for New York.

"We can't go," Nick said, a worried look on his face.

"I *have* to go. I have to be there."

And then I texted Therese: "Don't worry, I'm going to be there. I know you're going to be excited and busy with the event, so I'll leave you alone for now and will chat with Carl if I need any help. See you Friday!"

On Friday morning we woke up to the expected blanket of snow that covered the city and brought everything to a standstill. I half expected the event to be canceled, but everyone decided to forge ahead regardless of the weather. Each and every extra day Therese had in this world was priceless, and no snowstorm would stop any of us from being there for her on the occasion of her grand debut!

That morning, as I sipped on some tea and gathered my strength for the first outing since my surgery, I was surprised by an in-home mani-pedi and blowout, a gift from two wonderful and compassionate friends that I will never forget.

Such a gesture showed more love and understanding than any words could express. Something so simple meant the world to me and showed me how much they both cared.

Once I was prepped and ready to go, Nick tried one last time to change my mind. "Zulema, the snow is coming down hard outside," he said. "Imagine if you slip and fall and your incision opens up. Are you sure you want to go through with this?"

But I wasn't taking no for an answer, and he knew it. We left our house and carefully made our way to Grand Central Terminal, where we hopped on the train to Connecticut, then took an Uber to the venue. After the ninety-minute journey during which I remained standing or kneeling because I could not sit down, I was already exhausted but thrilled that we had made it, snowstorm notwithstanding.

We entered the gallery. It was like a sea of warmth amid the turbulent snowstorm roaring outside. It was packed. Seeing Therese's photos gracefully hanging from the walls filled my heart with joy—a feeling I hadn't really experienced over the past few weeks. The setup was perfect and the venue was pulsing with a sold-out crowd. The only person missing an hour into the party was the guest of honor. Exhaustion and fatigue were creeping up on me. I was thrilled to be there, but deep down all I wanted was to give my dear friend a hug, our last hug ever, and then flee back home and into my bed. I was pushing myself way beyond my limit, but I had already made it this far and needed to see this through. Eventually I sought out Therese's sister-in-law and explained that I wasn't sure I would be able to hang on much longer. "What's going on? Why isn't she here yet?" I asked.

"Come with me for a second," she replied in a whisper.

"I'm going to take you to a private room where Carl is going to call you."

She showed me to the greenroom and I settled onto the sofa—horizontally—and waited for the phone to ring. When I picked up, as expected, it was Carl on the other end of the line.

"Zulema, I'm really sorry that I'm going to miss you tonight, but neither I nor Therese will be able to make it," he said with great care.

"Oh my God, what is it? What's happening?" I asked, my heart racing.

"We went to see the space this morning to oversee how everything was being set up, and when we got home, Therese had liver failure. We're at home. Therese is going to pass away any minute now," he whispered.

My heart shattered into pieces. A million thoughts rushed through my head. Why did these things always happen to the good guys? Why couldn't God have given her just one more day so she could have made it to her exhibition? How would Carl and the children cope? Was this how my life would end?

As I tried to make sense of his words and managed to say goodbye, I began to sob uncontrollably, devastated by a loss that hit so close to home. I could not bear facing the crowd outside or standing during another train ride home, so Nick called a car service. Nick climbed into the front passenger seat and I lay across the back seat, heartbroken, with tears puddling below my cheek as we were driven home. *Life is so incredibly fragile,* I kept thinking on our way back to the city. Therese had missed her big debut by a mere few hours.

She passed away later that night and I never had the chance to give her that last hug. I do not know what God's plan might have been, but I take comfort in understanding that she spent her last few weeks focused on something she was passionate about rather than on her looming death. She also left us all with an incredible message of love and hope—one that changed my outlook on my disease. That day I vowed to love hard, and live hard, despite the fact that I had a cancer diagnosis. I did not want to be the person who gets told to go home, to put her affairs in order, to say her goodbyes because she has only a few weeks to live—and then tries to do all the things she had put off for tomorrow.

I firmly believe that God and the universe brought Therese and me together for reasons neither of us could have ever imagined. As night turned into day, it was still hard to accept that her steely will and indomitable spirit were no longer in the physical world. Her passing was a very tough loss at a crucial moment in my life. Her sudden absence not only caused me great sorrow but also made me feel incredibly alone and fragile. Therese had passed away at forty-two—the same age as me. This was the first time I had come face-to-face with my own mortality. I felt closer to death than life, and solace was hard to come by. Nick did his best to comfort me. He was the only one who knew how deeply impacted I was by Therese's death.

I carried the heartbreak of Therese's loss with me for many days, until one morning I realized that wallowing in sadness was the last thing she would have wanted me to do, so I snapped myself out of it. I was more determined than ever before to pursue my own life list and live my life with passion, no matter how many days, weeks, or years I had left. There is no time like the present to start doing what makes you happy. Most importantly, I wanted to live the life I had imagined with Nick without wasting a single second.

Five days after Therese's death, I found myself sitting in front of the Memorial Sloan Kettering sarcoma oncologist. Nick had offered to take time off from work and accompany me, but I said it wasn't necessary. I clearly wasn't thinking straight.

The oncologist handed me a copy of the report and said, "Your sarcoma is a soft tissue; the subtype is SFT, a solitary fibrous tumor. It is in early stage one, which is a good thing. But you have positive margins, which makes the case a little more difficult, so you will have to be monitored every three months."

Stage one: good, I thought. *Positive margins: bad.*

"There is no chemotherapy available for your type of tumor, so your only treatment option is radiation. I am sorry that you have this rare cancer."

My mind went blank except for *God, I have cancer!*

My head was spinning, and I really didn't take in what the doctor was telling me, but it was a laundry list of what was to come next. Luckily, I was recording the visit so I could go back over the conversation later. I managed to send Nick a text while I changed into a patient's gown for the examination portion of the appointment.

"Come to Memorial Sloan Kettering ASAP. Cancer is confirmed."

Nick must have literally dropped everything to run over, because twenty minutes later he was charging through the door. Externally, I remained composed as I sat through the appointment, but internally I was crumbling. I was battered. Broken. When we walked out of the building, I collapsed into Nick's arms in utter dismay. This was it: we had the diagnosis that both of us had tried to push away and tried to not think about. I was officially a cancer patient.

"What do you want to do?" Nick asked as we left the building. My mind was overwhelmed by the deluge of information and thoughts of the appointments to come, the possible radiation treatment, and all the other uncertainties that my new diagnosis entailed. I desperately yearned for something to look forward to.

"Let's go get the outdoor dining set we've been looking at for the past year," I replied. Now that I think about it, Nick must have thought I was crazy to want to go out and buy an outdoor furniture set when I had just received a life-altering diagnosis. I am sure he also knew that I needed to do something "normal." Just like the day I rushed into Barneys to buy myself a pair of Chanel flats after I received the news from my colorectal oncologist that I needed surgery. It was not about retail therapy; it was about buying something that would allow me to continue being myself at a time when my body was in shambles. Plus, I needed flats. I could not wear heels for eight weeks postsurgery. I needed to avoid at all costs falling on my behind, otherwise there would be serious consequences.

So, on the day that I was finally told I had cancer, it was not just about outfitting our terrace with outdoor furniture. In reality what I was doing was preparing for what I thought would be a summer in New York spent in cancer treatment. If I couldn't travel anywhere for the next few months, I wanted to turn our terrace into a little oasis where we could rest, relax, and receive friends while I underwent radiation.

Nick hailed a cab. As we drove away from Memorial Sloan Kettering, I called my mom to break the latest news. Her immediate response was, "What day do you start radiation?"

Typical Mami: needing a plan of action, always the practical one, not one to dwell on emotions.

We wrapped up our afternoon of shopping—yes, we ordered a stunning outdoor dining table, able to seat ten—and headed over to Cosme, one of my favorite Mexican restaurants in the city, for dinner. When the sommelier came over to our table, the first thing I ordered was a glass of champagne. I had not been able to drink alcohol for the past two months because of the painkillers I had been on, and I was not sure if I would be allowed to drink while on radiation, so at that moment I yearned to sip my favorite bubbly and forget, if only for an instant, about one of the most traumatic days of my life.

Details of what followed in the next day or two have been completely erased from my mind. It's all shadows and apprehension. The more I read about sarcoma, the more panic-stricken I became. I thought there was no hope, only death, and I descended into a deep well of despair. All I wanted was to regain control of my life, to press the rewind button, but instead I was at a total loss as far as what my next steps should be.

What ensued was an endless lineup of appointments with different cancer specialists and constant independent research on my end. Worried about the possible spread of my cancer, because I had an enlarged thyroid, they took a biopsy of my thyroid gland. Yet another procedure, but this one was performed under a local anesthetic.

I felt that the responsibility was on my shoulders to solve my own puzzle. But my medical cyclone kept roiling: the head-and-neck oncologist emailed saying he was not able to rule out lymphoma in my thyroid from the biopsy.

As I sat through each appointment, I started to have

doubts as to whether Memorial Sloan Kettering was the right place for me. I was under the impression that the doctors' goal would be to ensure that I felt confident with my diagnosis and that together we would lay out a treatment plan. They would do their homework on my complex medical history prior to every appointment and help put my mind at ease.

Instead I began to feel like another medical number; it was driving me insane. I realized that Memorial Sloan Kettering is absolutely the best place for treatment if you are diagnosed with the more common cancers; their approach is targeted and highly successful. But I had sarcoma coupled with a host of other conditions. I needed an alternative, another place that could understand all my physical conditions and emotional needs and treat me comprehensively. But I knew that because of a lack of funding and the rarity of sarcoma cases, not many places had departments that specialized in my type of cancer.

I devoted every second of my life to becoming my own advocate. I knew there had to be someone who was the world's authority on sarcoma, and after a little research and contacting the World Health Organization, I found him: Dr. Lowes.

Dr. Lowes is the head of onco-pathology at the Dana-Farber Cancer Institute in Boston. I called his office and his assistant walked me through the process of sending my pathology slides for him to render his opinion. I knew that I wanted three pathologies done and that his report would be the one I would listen to.

When Nick came home from work every day, I would be sitting at my computer, searching the Internet for articles about sarcoma or with my head in the latest medical book I had purchased from Amazon. As I researched and went over everything that had happened to me, I came across an article in *JAMA: The Journal of the American Medical Association.*

According to the article, the FDA had estimated that 1 in 352 women undergoing a hysterectomy had undetected uterine sarcoma, including leiomyosarcoma. NYU had used a morcellator (like a blender that chops up food and vegetables) to remove the fibroids through my belly button. The FDA had issued a warning to avoid use of the morcellator procedure for hysterectomy surgeries so as not to spread undetected malignancies. I was now extremely concerned that the hysterectomy fibroids were, in fact, leiomyosarcoma. I had developed one sarcoma; what if there had been a leiomyosarcoma hiding among the fibroids? Could the morcellator procedure have inadvertently sliced up a malignant leiomyosarcoma, sending cancer cells throughout my body? I confided my worries and concern about my ongoing treatment with my friend Lisa and told her I desperately needed alternative advice. Lisa listened attentively and said she knew of two people who had dealt with types of rare cancers. Maybe I should speak to them . . .

Promising to reach out to both of them, she hung up, and thirty minutes later she sent me a text: "You won't believe this: one of my two friends, Geraldine, had sarcoma!" Her words were like a balm to my soul, and the fact that she had used the past tense—Geraldine had *had* sarcoma—made me feel a colossal rush of hope.

Later that day, I received an email from Geraldine herself, and within hours we were speaking on the phone. There was no time to waste. A fantastic sense of relief inundated me as she validated everything I was feeling over the course of our forty-five-minute conversation. Before hanging up, we made plans to meet up, along with our husbands, to talk some more.

They came over to our place the following afternoon, and left Nick and me silently stunned as they shared their story.

Ten years earlier, Geraldine had been given six months to live after being diagnosed with osteosarcoma in her right arm. Osteosarcoma is another type of sarcoma, a cancer of the bone. She was also misdiagnosed. Several doctors in New York told her they would have to amputate her arm in order to save her life, and she was ready to make that sacrifice, but her husband refused to believe that was the only form of treatment. As a doctor himself, he did extensive research and decided that MD Anderson Cancer Center would be her best bet. Together, they uprooted their Manhattan life and set up an apartment for her in Houston, where she would spend the following year fighting for her life. And she did it: she survived! She is a ten-year-plus malignant peripheral nerve sheath sarcoma survivor. Geraldine and her husband could not speak more highly of MD Anderson, and as we talked, Nick and I learned it was home to the nation's center of excellence for treatment of both bone and soft-tissue sarcomas. By the end of that life-changing night in early April and before going to bed, Nick and I had made up our minds: we must also uproot our lives and get to MD Anderson.

The next morning I rushed to send Geraldine an email sharing our decision and asked her whether she could put me in touch with someone at MD Anderson to get a consultation appointment. She contacted MD Anderson right away, assuring me, as my new angel of hope, that neither Nick nor I would be alone in this journey moving forward.

Within five days of our meeting, and after numerous phone calls, oceans of forms, and extracting the last few years of records from every doctor who had treated me, I was in

MD Anderson's system. Two days later I received my admission date: April 27, 2015. I knew all too well how hard it is to get into a cancer institution quickly. Geraldine had worked a bona fide miracle! My hope rose to new heights, something I had not felt in months. I placed all my trust in this new chapter of my sarcoma treatment.

Meanwhile, I was gifted with another unforgettable gesture of love and friendship. I had been obsessing over an off-Broadway play called *Hamilton*. One day in early April my friend Lisa surprised me with two tickets. On April 11, 2015, Nick and I set off on our first postsurgery date to the Public Theater to see *Hamilton*. It would be many months more before the show hit Broadway and went viral and global.

I was thrilled. It was the musical that I had been pining over for months. As we sat in our seats, I looked up and my heart froze. Sitting in the row right in front of us was none other than Daniel Craig, the *real* James Bond, with his wife, Rachel Weisz. OMG! OMG! I felt like doing cartwheels.

While we were planning the details of our James Bond–themed wedding, the movie *Skyfall*, starring Daniel Craig, was released. We loved the movie! I kept saying to Nick, "We have to meet Daniel Craig; we have to figure out a way to meet him." Our wedding had incorporated all the different James Bond movies: The save-the-date invitation was titled *Goldfinger*, the stag party theme was *Casino Royale*, the rehearsal dinner theme was from *The Spy Who Loved Me,* and of course the table names for the wedding dinner were the names of the twenty-five James Bond movies!

I needed to tell Daniel our story but didn't want to blow his cover. I wanted to respect his privacy and night out with his wife, as no one around us recognized him. I decided to write a note during intermission to let him know we were big fans, that our alter egos were Mr. and Mrs. Bond, that our wedding theme was James Bond, and that Nick's wedding tuxedo was the one he wore in *Skyfall*—made to measure by Tom Ford—plus, why it meant so much to meet the real James Bond right then and there.

I tapped on Daniel's shoulder during intermission to hand him the note. He chuckled as he read it. He turned to us, extended his hand to both of us, and said, "Nice to meet you," with his melting James Bond voice. He wished me well and thanked us for being James Bond fans. Then he turned around again with a big smile on his face and said to Nick, "That was a bloody expensive tuxedo. Sorry, mate!" Daniel was incredibly gracious. I was floating on air, too, because I accepted it as a sign from God that he was watching over us, telling us to continue believing in healing and visualization, and to know that everything was going to be okay.

That evening reminded me to keep my hope alive, to keep visualizing my biggest dreams, regardless of the hardships and goals, and not to give up in any of my fights. A few nights later, as Nick and I lay in bed discussing our upcoming trip to Houston and wondering if we were making the right choice, he turned to face me, grabbed my hand tightly, looked me straight in the eyes, and said, "We're going to give everything we've got to keep fighting. If we need to go to China for your health and well-being, we will."

Good thing we only had to go as far as Texas.

12

The Z Word

We travel not to escape life,
but for life not to escape us.

—ANONYMOUS

And so it began on April 27, 2015. The quest for answers and hope.

The trip did not start out smoothly. The Friday before we were due to travel to Houston, I received a call from a person in the MD Anderson business center who was responsible for my case, explaining that we would have to reschedule our visit because they were still waiting to receive the pathology results required for my first appointment. It is customary for the cancer institution to perform its own pathology. I had arranged for Memorial Sloan Kettering to send the tissue slides. They sent them, but they hadn't made their way where they were needed at MD Anderson, so the pathology work hadn't been done.

Furious, I hung up and then called every department number I could find online, but getting through to pathology is like contacting the White House—impossible! There was no way in hell I was going to delay my trip because someone had failed to do their job! I moved heaven and earth. Eventually, I got through to the head of patient affairs, and within a few hours the matter was rectified. One thing I have learned during my medical journey is to never take no for an answer. We were back on schedule.

The phone call was the last thing I had wanted to receive. The previous two weeks had been extremely stressful, pulling together the medical records MD Anderson needed—every MRI, scan, blood work, and medical record from the previous two years, organizing flights and hotel accommodations, and answering emails.

Yes, I appreciated the emails and calls from friends and family inquiring about my well-being, but once you have answered the same questions for the tenth time, it starts to become draining. I couldn't do it anymore. It was too much for me. I was overwhelmed. As I was packing for the upcoming trip, I made a decision: I would start a blog. The purpose would be threefold: to keep everyone updated on my situation, to share the wealth of information I was slowly uncovering to help others on a similar journey, and to find an outlet for my speeding thoughts and the emotional roller coaster I was on while navigating the dreaded C-word. And then it came to me: not the C-word; my blog would be *The Z Word*.

Most friends and family resisted and criticized this method of communication. Some felt offended when I directed them to the blog instead of answering their questions directly or talking to them. They didn't get it. They probably still don't get it. I know I don't handle questions well under stress. I didn't want to repeat myself a million times a day; I needed to quiet my mind and not relive the issues I was battling by going over them again and again. The lesson here is if someone is dealing with a cancer diagnosis, don't just text or call to ask, "How are you?" Be more supportive by asking what you can do to help, or even better, doing something you know will make a positive difference for them.

I wanted to write as much as I could about what I was experiencing. I didn't want to forget the details of my journey. I had no plans to write a book at that very moment, but deep down I knew that someday I would get to tell my story. This would be my journal. If what I wrote about offended people, then so be it. As I began what I hoped would be the final quest for answers, I wanted to keep a detailed record of the medicines I would take and treatment I would undergo and how I reacted to them. This proved invaluable later on in my treatment. Last but certainly not least, I wanted to reach out and connect with other people who might be going through what I was going through or had just started finding out about that rare vascular "thing" reported on their MRI.

April 25, 2015

*I am beginning a new chapter in my quest to beat sarcoma
and get to the bottom of all my health issues. I need a
holistic approach to my health care. I am fervently hoping
that I will find that at MD Anderson. I want nothing more
than to be treated by an integrated team of doctors and
oncologists under one roof. Memorial Sloan Kettering has
fantastic individual medical professionals, but I need a
seamless team fighting on my side to understand the array
of medical conditions that plague my body. I not only
have soft-tissue sarcoma, a rare cancer in its own right,
but also a rare solitary fibrous tumor in a rare location
on my body—a triple whammy—plus gastroparesis
and Hashimoto's thyroiditis. I await tests for possible
lymphoma of the thyroid and I have an undiagnosed
eye issue . . . I need professionals who can work together
and look at my body as a whole to understand if or how*

*one illness or condition interacts with another. And most
importantly, find out where they stem from. What is
causing all this?*

*I am excited and nervous at the same time: excited
that I might at long last get the answers I am looking for
but nervous that this might end up at another dead end.
And then there is the impact on my husband. He is going
to work from Houston during my treatment. He puts a
good face on it, but I know he is worried about being away
from the office for such an extended period. Investment
banking is a tough world and I know you have to be at the
top of your game all the time. It's not just his salary we rely
on, but, now with a pre-existing condition, my continued
treatment depends on the healthcare benefits that come
with Nick's job. We're in this together.*

April 26, 2015

*I am writing this as I sit on the Jet Blue flight to Houston.
I feel a sense of normalcy by being up here, looking out
over friendly skies. Nick and I love to travel. It's one of the
things that drew us together initially. Even though our final
destination this time is far from the vacation destination
of our dreams, we have both decided to treat this as an
opportunity to explore a city that has not been on our radar
or life list but will become our second home for the next few
weeks and maybe even the next few years.*

Sunday Evening, April 26, 2015

*We landed at Houston's William B. Hobby Airport, and as
we made our way to the baggage claim, I was overcome with
tears at the sight of a massive MD Anderson billboard that*

proclaimed, "One goal: ~~cancer~~." I couldn't help but squeeze Nick's hand tightly. I was awash in optimism and hope.

We have now arrived at our home for the foreseeable future: the Hotel ZaZa. It is a beautiful art-filled space recommended by my new friend Geraldine. Having been through this process herself, she suggested we stay here instead of the hotel on the MD Anderson premises, where you cannot help but live and breathe cancer both day and night. We are only a ten-minute drive away from the center: close enough to get to appointments easily, but far enough away to have a break from the hospital gowns, IVs, and other patients. They even provide a fancy Cadillac Escalade with bulls' horns for a front bumper to transport us to and from the MD Anderson buildings when needed. Perfect accommodations!

Monday, April 27, 2015

Nobody can quite grasp the immensity of MD Anderson unless you've actually been there in person. It's like a city within a city, with street after street and building after building dedicated to researching and eliminating cancer and offering care to its more than 100,000 patients. At first it is quite intimidating and overwhelming, but then you realize that this monumental establishment is there to help you and it quickly becomes a place of hope and comfort. I walked those hallways today, our first day here, my focus on finding the care I so desperately need, praying I will land in good hands, putting my faith in God and this institution. No medical institution is like MD Anderson. Today they took blood samples and did routine tests. Tomorrow I begin my appointments in earnest and, with God's will, find the path to stable future health.

There were many nights Nick would hold me tight in bed and tell me that no matter what happened, I was the love of his life, that he was proud of me for tackling my disease, without being a victim, and how he admired that I had the guts to fight a system that's not designed to help the patient.

Tuesday Morning, April 28, 2015
I was incredibly anxious last night. I couldn't eat dinner.
I tossed and turned in bed. I don't know what to expect; I
don't know if I can allow myself to feel any kind of hope.
Does my case come with hope or is it a death sentence?
I am impatient to learn more but afraid of what new
knowledge might reveal.

Tuesday Evening, April 28, 2015
My first appointment of the day was with Dr. Linda Smith,
the sarcoma surgical oncologist assigned to my case who
would also serve as the main point person for my case. I
knew the first thing I needed to discuss with her. The surgeon
at Memorial Sloan Kettering had suggested I undergo
radiation after surgery to kill off any lingering cancer cells.
But when I spoke to the radiation oncologist at Memorial
Sloan Kettering, he said, "Given the location and type of
tumor, I don't recommend it." He went on to tell me the side
effects could range from bladder deformation, colitis, and
rectum incontinence, to vaginal tissue distortion that would
make sex painful. I asked him what the bad news was! I
was anxious to hear Dr. Smith's take on the matter.
I came prepared to the appointment with a clinical
summary document I developed to avoid repeating myself
over and over again and forgetting things such as how

many surgeries I had been through, what meds I was on, what were my symptoms, and what the most recent tests I had had were. My clinical summary document has six pages' worth of data, including family cancer history (which is very prevalent on my dad's side).

Dr. Smith didn't recommend radiation treatment, either, for my type of sarcoma. Knowing there is an 80 percent possibility that my sarcoma could recur in the first two years, she recommended imaging and checkups every three months for the next two to three years. I explained my frustration with the Memorial Sloan Kettering system back home and that I was seeking comprehensive care under one roof. After reading through my medical summary and records, she said she believed most of my symptoms were related to chronic autoimmune diseases. At this point the only autoimmune disease I had been diagnosed with was Hashimoto's thyroiditis and of course a brief diagnosis of lupus, though it was my understanding that it had been temporary. But she said diseases, plural; she suspects there are more to be discovered. Great—just what I need to look forward to!

After that first day of appointments, Nick and I went out to dinner and of course ordered a bottle of Pierre Peters Les Chétillons 2000 champagne. Champagne is always the answer. We were both relieved, but for different reasons. I was relieved that I was finally getting some of the answers I had been look-ing for. He was relieved because he heard Dr. Smith say that I would not need radiation. He figured that on the sarcoma front we were all done. It was simply a question of monitoring my health to make sure the sarcoma did not recur. Frustrated by what I considered to be his naïveté, I explained that we still had quite a few hurdles to get over. I think this was the first argument we ever had regarding my health. Suffice it to say, the tension was high that evening. Nick is the eternal optimist, whereas I have learned to be skeptical of everything and everyone. I needed more time to let everything sink in. I didn't want to rush to conclusions and think I was out of the woods until we had met all the doctors and completed all the tests. We finished our awkward dinner and headed back to the hotel.

> *Wednesday, April 29, 2015*
>
> *Today I had a thyroid biopsy, I am scheduled to see an endocrinology later in the week, and I was told that MD Anderson's pathology report agreed with the Memorial Sloan Kettering and Dana Farber pathologies. That is great news! There are now no more doubts about my sarcoma: I had a stage 1, low-grade solitary fibrous tumor, albeit with positive margins. This information certainly brings some peace of mind, but I still felt uneasy about the unknown. Dr. Smith said earlier today that, in her twenty years of treating sarcoma patients, she had seen only four or five other cases like my own and thought my chances were good, but she couldn't speak with certainty, as every case is different.*

For the rest of the week, I ticked off ten or more appointments and tests in gastroenterology, OB-GYN, ophthalmology, the undiagnosed breast clinic, head-and-neck department, neurology, and genetics. You name it, I had it done. I felt like a car getting a thorough look over from the engine to the trunk. I have never experienced such detailed and thorough care in my life, and I thanked Dr. Smith every day for looking out for me.

Every day we would start at five in the morning. Nick

would get up to do work video calls from his laptop. We would then have a light breakfast; many times I could not eat, often from nerves, and sometimes because of the tests or procedure scheduled for later in the day. By this point I had dropped to between a size 0 and a size 2, but I certainly wouldn't advocate my experience as a weight-loss program. When we got to the hospital, I was shown into the first waiting room, where I would change into that pair of blue scrubs that would be my attire for the day—very Chanel! While I was being prodded and examined, Nick would sit in the waiting area, often on yet more video calls as he tried to continue to do his job remotely. Three to four appointments and at least one procedure were scheduled each day. Meanwhile, I was constantly surrounded by fellow cancer patients, many in much worse condition than me, teetering on the brink of death and walking around in hospital gowns hooked up to their chemo machines. While waiting my turn at the lab, a very ill man collapsed onto the floor. The nurses immediately called a "code red," but before anyone could help, I watched him take his last few breaths—right there in front of me. Talk about putting everything into perspective! All my energy was focused on getting through each hour, each painful test, each new result.

The daily routine usually ended at around four in the afternoon, after which we would go out for an early dinner and then retire to our room to rest, make calls, review a sea of emails, write my blog, and prepare to do it all over again the following morning. On one such early evening, we headed to Prego, the local Italian eatery, for our usual meal at the bar, and ordered a glass of champagne for me and a Rinaldi Barolo for Nick. We liked to sit at the bar to interact with other people, make small talk, distract ourselves, and possibly make new friends in town. While we sipped our drinks, a woman and man in their fifties sat next to us and we struck up a conversation. The woman had noticed I was wearing the infamous bracelet that identified me as an MD Anderson patient. I noticed the blue cross and burns peaking above her strapless top, which likely meant she was undergoing radiation for breast cancer, but she had no bracelet. It turned out she was getting treated for breast cancer at Houston Methodist. We immediately hit it off and ended up exchanging contact info. Before leaving, they reassured Nick, who had to leave in a few days' time for urgent meetings in London he had to be present at, that they would take care of me while he was gone.

They left and we stayed on a little longer chatting, and when it came time to pay the bill, we were stunned to realize that they had taken care of it for us. Tears flooded my eyes and I immediately called them to thank them for such a generous and spontaneous act of kindness. It was the first time something like that had ever happened to us, and during such a gut-wrenching time in our lives, it truly left us speechless. Suffice it to say we are still friends to this day and meet up with them each time we go to Houston. I made sure to pay it forward three days later to a single mom who was my Uber driver. As we drove to MD Anderson, I learned our driver's mom was in critical condition at MD Anderson; she had three small children and was struggling financially. At the end of the ride, I gave her every dollar I had in my wallet. She was speechless and crying as I handed her the bills. Almost everyone you meet in Houston around the MD Anderson area has been touched in one way or another by cancer. There is an unspoken camaraderie and compassion among people you meet and that can make all the difference in the world.

Friday, May 1, 2015

I had lunch today with Dr. Smith and Dr. Gomez, a
sarcoma surgical oncologist and the head scientist
leading the soft-tissue sarcoma investigative laboratory
at MD Anderson. Dr. Smith thought it would be a great
idea for me to meet Dr. Gomez, as we are both Puerto
Rican women and united by sarcoma! I asked Dr. Gomez
so many questions regarding sarcoma. She readily
answered all of them and invited me to visit her lab. I
will definitely take her up on her offer. There is so much
I don't really know about sarcoma, but there are so
many sub-types, even the scientists admit there is still so
much to investigate, it was fascinating to meet a young
Latina woman on the forefront of sarcoma research.

The first weekend in Houston was blessed with beautiful
spring weather, which we took advantage of by taking a long
walk in Hermann Park. The relentless schedule spent indoors,
sprinting from one appointment to another, left us yearning for
some fresh air and different scenery. We strolled down one of the
lanes surrounded by lush green trees, found a bench adjacent to
the placid McGovern Lake, and sat side by side, observing pedal
boats swish by and listening to birds chirping above our heads.

We began an hours-long conversation about my options and
best path ahead. I can still remember that afternoon as if it were
yesterday. Dr. Smith had closed the week by telling us that it was
time for us to decide whether MD Anderson would be my main
treatment clinic for all follow-up scans. It is advisable that anyone with cancer pick one institution for their care permanently
and not jump from one to another. We were also very much
aware that choosing MD Anderson meant choosing to be in

Houston for at least one week every three months for my follow-up scans and treatment, which would be a big undertaking.

Nick and I carefully weighed the pros and cons. We also crunched the numbers to see what level of financial commitment was necessary while trying to be as realistic as possible with the best- and worst-case scenarios we might face in the future. Nick would not be able to come to every visit given his job. However, when all was said and done, we voted yes to make MD Anderson our official treatment center. It was the obvious choice.

"Let's do this," Nick said. "Your health has to take precedence."

In that short week, I felt more comfortable with the care I received from MD Anderson than from any other medical institution before. Whatever sacrifices were necessary to make it work out were worth it.

The following two weeks were more of the same: appointments, exams, eat, sleep, and repeat. Nick had to fly back to New York and then to London for work, so a friend flew in from New York to stay with me the following weekend, and then I was left alone. I missed Nick terribly. He needed to take care of his job. I needed to take care of my health. The one thing I knew I would not accept was the possibility of spending our second anniversary, May 17, 2015, apart. I needed to be by his side, feel his warm embrace, and celebrate our union together.

I left Houston with answers to many of my medical questions. The thyroid biopsy had proven negative. I didn't have cancer of the eye: the antibody test for cancer-associated retinopathy had also come back negative. However, I would have to have my eyes monitored regularly during my quarterly checkups.

I had tested positive for paraneoplastic syndrome, a disorder triggered by an altered immune system. The specialist thought the disorder and altered immune system were probably the result of my sarcoma and not the early stages of eye cancer.

I had much more peace of mind. I felt I had the dream team looking out for me now, a team I would be seeing every three months. Nick was still in England, so when I got to JFK, I swapped airlines for a flight to London. We didn't have a big celebration, or a fancy dinner planned for our anniversary. Just being together was enough for me. We spent time with Nick's son John, took in a James Bond exhibition, ate brunch at our private member club, 67 Pall Mall, and enjoyed having the weight lifted off our shoulders.

When I returned to New York, I had to come to grips with my Hashimoto's thyroiditis and the suspicion that many of my health conditions were likely stemming from other autoimmune diseases. Dr. Smith recommended I see a rheumatologist in New York. Although the idea was to have all my care under one roof, when it came to rheumatology, it was best to keep that local, as I would need constant treatment.

When my blood work came back, my new rheumatologist, Dr. Frances, told me that my antinuclear antibody (ANA) levels were very high and that I had lupus. This did not come as a big surprise, but the reality of it hit me like a ton of bricks. She recommended methotrexate, a chemotherapy agent to suppress my immune system and restore my ANA levels to normal range. I honestly had thought I had dodged the chemo bullet. I had dodged it with my sarcoma diagnosis, but my autoimmune disease had other ideas. What worried me the most were the possible side effects. Chemo . . . Would I lose my hair?

Tuesday June 30, 2015

Lisa invited us upstate for the Fourth of July, but I don't
know if I can handle being in a car or on a bus for several
hours with the bouts of nausea I am having from the
methotrexate. It is hard to get up in the morning, I am tired
all the time, I lack energy and an appetite. I freak out when
I find hair on my pillowcase and in the shower—balls of
hair. I made an appointment with a wig shop the other day
but never followed through. My sarcoma seems to be under
control. I just need to figure out how to deal with my lupus.

That summer Nick had to make a business trip to London
in August and did not want to leave me home alone. I had
been on my weekly chemo routine now for two months and
my body was slowly beginning to adapt to the methotrexate
I was subjecting it to every Sunday evening. I was less tired,
and my energy and appetite had returned. My hair continued
to thin, but it didn't appear like I was going to go bald. A new
set of hair extensions hid most of the evidence. Eventually, I
ended up chopping off my hair above my shoulders. A bold
move and certainly a different look to my signature long flow-
ing locks! I wanted to accompany him on the trip. I knew he
needed a break from the stress of supporting me during my
treatment at MD Anderson while at the same time holding
down his job. We needed to take a trip and at the same time
tick off another item on our life list.

Istanbul in August, before Nick had to be in London, was
our answer.

13

Artz Cure Sarcoma

*In order to be irreplaceable
one must always be different.*

—COCO CHANEL

On July 20, 2015, two weeks before our trip to Istanbul, a suicide attack in Suruc, Turkey, claimed by ISIS, killed 34 people and injured 103. The city was on high alert. Many of our friends urged us to err on the side of caution and cancel our plans, but we refused to be intimidated by terrorism. They all thought we were crazy to forge ahead, but no one but the two of us could truly understand how our life had changed—not to mention how our outlook on life had changed. Friends, family, work, and life balance—our priorities were turned on their head. I often thought that if I were to die from a terrorist attack while visiting Istanbul, at least everyone would find comfort in knowing that I died doing something I loved and wanted to do. I cannot comprehend why people are driven by fear, because it prevents them from living their best life possible. When you put out fear or negativity to the universe, the universe hears you and returns back fear and negativity. During this trip, Nick and I renewed our vow that from that moment on—come rain, shine, cancer, or no cancer, no matter what others thought—we would live in the present. Not the past or the future.

From the time we arrived in Istanbul, I felt a sense of belonging, as if I had lived there in a previous life. It transported us to a magnificent place where we learned about another impressive city's culture, history, wine, cuisine, and traditions. We had two of the most romantic dinner dates in our eight years together, and magically, for a few days, Istanbul washed away our worries and replenished us with energy, love, and life.

The clear headedness resulting from our journey also gave way to a terrific and inspired idea that has since changed my life, not to mention given me a new and fulfilling sense of purpose. It also became my own way of coping with my sarcoma and all my illnesses and conditions. It had been brewing in my mind for a while, ever since the phone conversation I had had with Lisa about the two people we knew who had rare cancers: one had written a book about their experience, and the other, my friend Geraldine, was making a documentary about sarcoma.

My idea? With my advertising and marketing background, I was going to create awareness of sarcoma. How? I would first gather all my friends and business acquaintants for a cocktail evening at our place to get the ball rolling. Many had asked how they could help. Well, this was their opportunity by learning about sarcoma and spreading awareness of the disease. I wanted to impact the course of the disease and make it a life mission, because my inner voice and gut said I was chosen to get this type of cancer.

Until then, the deep research I had done on sarcoma was related to my type of sarcoma, but I was curious to learn more about sarcoma overall, both soft-tissue and osteosarcoma, and I wanted to visit the sarcoma lab at MD Anderson to see a live sarcoma cell and meet the people who devoted their lives to investigating the disease and thank them for their hard work.

As I dove into full sarcoma research mode in light of my new passion project, I quickly realized that this was not only a rare and orphan cancer but also one of the deadliest forms of cancer in children and adults. Let me give you the quick, cumulative rundown on what I know. Sarcoma is a malignant tumor that can grow in any type of connective tissue—cells that connect or support other kinds of tissue in your body. Sarcoma is not a single disease, as it has more than seventy different subtypes. It's a family of related diseases rather than a single specific disease.

Sarcomas are divided into two categories:

- Soft-tissue sarcoma
- Osteosarcoma, also known as bone sarcoma

Soft-tissue sarcomas can develop in body fat, muscles, blood vessels, tendons, nerves and fibrous tissues, and synovial tissues (tissues around the joints). According to the National Cancer Institute, there are approximately 11,280 new cases of soft-tissue sarcoma in the United States every year, and about 3,900 people die of the disease each year. About 40 percent occur in the legs usually at or above the knee. Fifteen percent develop in the hands and arms, 15 percent in the head and neck, and 30 percent in the shoulders, chest, abdomen, or hips.

Osteosarcoma occurs in the bone or cartilage. These tumors can develop in any part of the body, including the extremities, head, neck, internal organs, abdomen, and the back of the abdomen. Osteosarcoma is very rare, with about 2,890 new cases diagnosed in the United States each year, and approximately 1,410 deaths.

Sarcomas are often named according to the normal-tissue cells they most closely resemble. I had a solitary fibroid tumor. This is different from most other types of cancer, which are usually named for the part of the body where the cancer began.

Sarcoma rarely causes symptoms in the early stages. The first sign of a sarcoma in an arm, or a leg, may be a painless lump or swelling. Because sarcomas can develop in flexible, elastic tissues or deep spaces in the body, the tumor can often easily push normal tissue out of its way as it grows; which is what happened to me. Therefore, a sarcoma may grow quite large before it causes symptoms. Eventually, it may cause pain as the growing tumor begins to press against nerves or muscles.

Sarcoma is a very dangerous disease because not only does it rarely cause symptoms in early stages, most sarcomas don't have identifiable risk factors. There are no routine screening tests recommended or preventive measures, such as regular mammogram screenings for breast cancer or colonoscopies for colon cancer.

Given that it is such a rare and complex form of cancer, there is no financial incentive for the government or pharmaceutical companies to invest in research and treatment, which leaves those of us diagnosed with this disease in dire circumstances. Sarcoma research is virtually nonexistent due to the lack of funding, which means no new treatments are being developed—a major contributor to poor survival rates.

In other words, sarcoma patients do not have targeted therapies or chemo drugs like other cancer sufferers. Eighty percent of sarcomas recur within the first two years of diagnosis—much higher than other cancers. Sarcoma very often metastasizes in the lungs. Once sarcoma has spread to another part of the body, the prognosis is very poor. Last but not least, there is a massive lack of awareness about sarcoma. There is no Angelina Jolie, Rita Wilson, or other high-profile celebrity with sarcoma who can help boost an awareness of the disease through their own journey.

Knowing all this and aware that information is power, I could not stand by and do nothing; the impulse to power change was strong. A voice inside told me to pursue this further. I have always been committed to helping others, but this was much bigger than me. I wanted to not only raise awareness, but fund research, be a patient advocate, and help save lives.

During one of the most romantic dinners Nick and I have ever had, overlooking the Asian side of Turkey on a stunning outdoor terrace, and sharing a bottle of Turkish Cabernet Sauvignon, I shared my desire to act. First I suggested making an individual donation to Dr. Gomez to aid her invaluable sarcoma research. But as we continued to brainstorm ways to raise money, everything seemed to circle back to our love of hosting lavish parties with our friends and my flair for event planning. Why not throw one of our memorable year-end parties? We would serve bottomless champagne all night and provide the ambiance for people to mingle and network. But this time there would be a twist: instead of bringing the usual bottle of wine to the party, we would ask for a donation to fund sarcoma research. This would surely surpass our idea of an individual donation from us and help raise sarcoma awareness among our friends and acquaintances. Nick was sold on the idea, and we continued to brainstorm while enjoying our time in Istanbul.

Once we were back home in September, I started bouncing

this idea off friends to see who might be willing to pitch in. Then suddenly there was that inner voice again!

Earlier in the year I had commissioned an Albert Einstein piece from the artist Kfir Moyal; however, when it was delivered, it was damaged. He kindly made a new one, which proudly hangs at home to this day, but I had yet to return the damaged one. I wondered: Might Kfir be willing to donate it for a silent auction benefiting sarcoma? Then the wheels started turning, and I wondered whether other artists we collected might also be willing to donate a piece. We could have a silent auction. Everyone I approached with the idea readily agreed to participate, and within three weeks what began as a simple desire to host a fun party to benefit my cause became a full-blown event with a silent auction boasting more than twenty pieces of art, including my favorite piece by my deceased friend Therese from her exhibition.

As the day of the fund-raiser neared, I talked to my friend Geraldine and told her I was in awe of all the support I was getting. I did not expect such a turnout.

"I think you're onto something. You will create a movement for sarcoma," she said.

She was right. One day, sitting on the terrace with Geraldine and Nick, we started brainstorming about a name for the upcoming party so that it would make a clear statement for all those participating and attending. It had to have the word *sarcoma* in it, and since it was based on an art auction, *art* should also be mentioned in the theme or title. Then Nick exclaimed, "How about Arts Cure Sarcoma?"

I loved it, but I knew it was still missing something. I wanted the name to have a component that reflected the person behind this rising movement, a human element, a face that others could relate to. I was not just organizing this fund-raiser; I had also been directly affected by this rare cancer. That was when Nick said, "Let's replace the *s* in *Arts* with a *z* to represent your name," and the decision was made.

I designed a quick logo, which was later redone by a professional, and that is how Artz Cure Sarcoma was born. It was a party turned fund-raiser turned movement that would eventually become a nonprofit foundation. It only goes to show how brainstorming an idea, no matter how insignificant you may think it is, can become a calling, a purpose, that goes beyond your wildest dreams.

Planning for the event took up most of my free time. It served as a fantastic coping mechanism and full-time distraction, until it was once again time for my three-month checkup at MD Anderson in October. And of course anxiety paid a visit. Pre-checkup anxiety can be so overpowering that it actually has a name: *scanxiety*. If you google this term, you get more than 40,000 results. Most people who have or have had cancer agree that some of the most terrifying moments of their lives occurred in the days and hours leading up to the scans that told them if they were in the clear or if their cancer was back. As the date of my checkup neared, my brain slowly shifted into another dimension, my other life, where hope and fear collided. The trepidation of a positive result overshadowed all reasoning. As if this trepidation alone were not enough, I had continued having bouts of anal bleeding for months following my sarcoma surgery, and I knew from my June appointment with my MD Anderson colorectal oncologist that this likely meant a new surgery was on the horizon.

I spent the second week of October at MD Anderson in a gown or scrubs, on a wheelchair, gurney, or exam table, undergoing an array of appointments, scans, procedures, and biopsies. Thank God for warm blankets! The days were long and harrowing, but eventually all the scan results came back clear with "No Evidence of Disease"—NED. Three simple letters that I prayed to hear. I could live and plan out the next three months.

However, I did learn that the bouts of bleeding that I still suffered from were due to anal fissures requiring attention. My colorectal oncologist delivered the news: I would need another surgery. It did not come as a surprise, but it was something I had hoped I could avoid. We scheduled the intervention for November 16 so that I could host my fund-raising event before surgery. This would be my thirteenth surgery in my forty-two years, the second that year, and the fourth in the previous year and a half.

When I got back home, I channeled all my energy into making the first Artz Cure Sarcoma event a success. I was determined to raise the most money I could. I also wanted my friends and acquaintances to walk away with a greater understanding of sarcoma and more aware of the uncertainties I faced. This was also a way for everyone who told me "Let me know what I can do" to actually get involved and help.

We hit the ball out of the park. The outpouring of support was amazing. Our neighbors helped hang art on our terrace for the evening. All our friends and guests who attended bid on the artwork. Luis D. Ortiz, my friend and former personality from Bravo's *Million Dollar Listing New York*, was the MC for the evening. We ended up raising a grand total of $45,000—more than we had expected—which we donated to the investigative laboratory led by Dr. Gomez at MD Anderson and Geraldine's documentary, *Until 20*, which told the story of James Ragan and his journey with osteosarcoma.

My heart was bursting from the event. I was able to set aside my Artz Cure Sarcoma duties with a huge smile on my face to prepare for my upcoming surgery. Even though I knew this would not be a complicated or life-threatening procedure, going under and waking up to the pangs of recovery pain is never easy. Anal surgery is by far the worst type of surgery. Anxiety also creeps up on me and tears never fail to fill my eyes when I say goodbye to Nick as I am rolled into the OR; there is always that fear it may be the last time we see each other. While the procedure went as well as it could, there were still some growths that could not be removed. "I didn't want to remove all the growths," the surgeon told me while I was in recovery. "It would have meant removing more of your anal muscle. If I ever have to go back in and do a further sarcoma resection, you could lose all of your anal muscle and you certainly don't want that."

As with my first sarcoma surgery, I was not allowed to sit for the following five weeks, and the pain was similar. But I took comfort in knowing that if I had been able to survive the discomfort once, I could do it again. The underlying concern with each of these surgeries was permanent side effects.

One day while I was recovering, I feared the worst had arrived. I was in bed resting, when I suffered a small burst of incontinence. I rushed to the bathroom, worried sick, recalling that the doctor had mentioned that such a side effect could become a chronic issue. I began to sob. Here I was, a vibrant forty-two-year-old young woman facing issues normally encountered by the elderly. I was scared. But as the days passed, it did not recur, and I once again breathed a deep sigh of relief. I spent Thanksgiving at home in bed and in pain.

Throughout the entire sarcoma ordeal in 2015, Nick and I had a lot of time to talk about our lives, where we were going, what we most wanted. We often revisited our life list, but I felt stuck in the limbo between recovering from one health issue and dealing with the next one that came along. Nick knew I needed something to take my mind off my illnesses. As we spoke further, a fun idea emerged: enrolling in wine school.

Studying wine had been on our life list from the get-go. In fact, back in December 2013, I had gifted Nick with a wine class at one of the New York sommelier schools as a birthday present. And so in March 2016 we enrolled in evening classes with the Wine & Spirit Education Trust (WSET). We set ourselves the ambitious goal of completing the Diploma level, a qualification recognized as an actual diploma by the New York Department of Education and equivalent to a bachelor's degree in wine.

That was hands down one of the best decisions we have ever made as husband and wife! The wine world has introduced us to a great circle of friends and people of all walks of life. Wanting to capture our wine-tasting memories, but conscious that our other friends and family might be critical of such an activity given my health, we decided to set up an anonymous Instagram account. But what to call it? It didn't take look for us to come up with the name—BondSomms. If you ask around the wine world, people may not have heard of Nick and Zulema, but they surely know BondSomms. We haven't received our diploma yet, but we did finish WSET Levels 1, 2, and 3. We still have unfinished business.

By the end of 2016, Nick knew he needed a break from his job. The stress of holding down a managing director role at a Wall Street firm while at the same time taking time out to support me and my treatment had been hard on him. In October 2016, following a reorganization at his firm, he decided to take a break from Wall Street and quit his job. We wanted to spend time together that didn't involve hospital wards or doctors' offices. Traveling to the different wine regions of the world, to understand the terroir, to meet the vineyard owners, producers, to learn hands-on about viticulture, and witness winemaking techniques in action had bubbled to the top of our life list.

Interspersed with the mandatory three-month checkups at MD Anderson, we spent the next twelve months ticking off one wine region after the next. First stop: traveling down the west coast of North America, from Sonoma and Napa, through Sta. Rita Hills, Paso Robles, and Santa Barbara all way down to the Valle de Guadalupe in Mexico. Next up: Bordeaux, followed by Ribera del Duero and Rioja. Then on to Italy: Piedmont, Tuscany, and Bolgheri. And yes, we got to meet all our favorite producers—Harlan Estate, Colgin, Latour, Pétrus, Vega Scilia, Chiara Boschis, Giuseppe Rinaldi, and Ornellaia, just to name a few.

But my favorite part of our wine tour was spending time in Champagne. I am very fortunate to have forged close bonds and friendships with many of the producers whose wines we collect. No matter what, everything seems better with champagne! Since our first trip in 2010, I have been back a further eight times, each time learning more about the region, meeting new producers, and getting together for dinners with the close friends I have made in that chalk-filled land.

But 2016 didn't only kick off our wine adventures; an evening in March truly launched Artz Cure Sarcoma. After failing to get tickets to Adele's Madison Square Garden concerts, tickets on her 2016 European tour became available and we jumped at the opportunity to see her in her hometown of London. We scored tickets to her last concert of the European tour at the O$_2$ arena.

I had Artz Cure Sarcoma constantly on my mind. After that first successful fund-raiser, I established Artz Cure Sarcoma as a business, registering it as an LLC on the advice of an attorney who said turning it into a foundation would be a much bigger undertaking and a much harder entity to dissolve if it did not work out in the long run. I was sure Nick and I could take it to the next level, but I wasn't sure how. I needed and asked for a signal from the spiritual world, from my dad and the angels, every night when I went to bed. I wanted a sign that would show me I was on the right path and shouldn't abandon the idea.

Five days before the Adele concert, Nick was asked to attend a senior executive meeting in Switzerland. It was scheduled for the same day as the show. I couldn't believe our bad luck, but there was truly nothing he could do. I suggested we get tickets for the Monday concert so we could go together regardless, and then I would use our Tuesday tickets to take a friend who had introduced me to Adele's music back in 2009. I was unaware that this decision would impact my life in unimaginable ways.

During the Monday night concert, after the second song, Adele stopped the music to chitchat with the audience and be her usual adorable self. That is when I noticed it: signs everywhere. It seemed the audience knew this break would happen and many of them were prepared. Adele glanced around and spied a sign held by a young woman standing two rows in front of us. It was her twenty-fifth birthday. Adele encouraged the entire arena to sing "Happy Birthday" to her. I was in total awe of the moment, when suddenly that voice inside me piped up: *Bring your own sign tomorrow.* Nick laughed and laughed at my idea, but my mind was made up. It was somewhat normal for people to laugh at my ideas or not take me seriously. All I wanted was a selfie, and never in my wildest dreams did I imagine what would happen next!

For the concert on Tuesday, April 5, 2016, I bought poster boards, taped them together, rolled them up, and put a marker in my purse, thinking I would write my message to her once I met my friend for drinks prior to the concert. I definitely wanted Adele to know I had come from New York to see her, but I also had to add something catchy enough to compel her to pick my sign over the sea of others. As I brainstormed with my friend, she said, "Why don't you add that you're a cancer survivor?" I was hesitant at first, not wanting to use my plight as an attention-getter but added it at the last minute. The sign said:

NYC → LONDON
FOR ADELE!!
BUCKET LIST ✔
CANCER SURVIVOR
LOVE YOU ADELE!

I eagerly waited for her second song, "Hometown Glory," to end in order to spring into action. When Adele started talking, I jumped out of my aisle seat and held up my sign, heart pounding with excitement and anticipation. Suddenly, Adele turned my way and then, much to my disbelief and thrill, I heard her say, "Oh, that's a nice sign," and proceeded to read it out loud. "Well, come on over!"

Wait, I thought. *She wants me to come to the stage?* Trembling from head to toe, I rushed down the walkway to the front of the arena. My eyes were clouded over with tears as I took the final step to meet her up onstage, the sound of the entire O₂ arena cheering me on in my ears.

"You look very glamorous. Is that a Balmain × H&M coat? I couldn't even get one for myself," she said, and then gave me a big, warm hug while my tears turned into rain on her shoulder. She made me feel at ease with her—we were laughing, bantering onstage about my Puerto Rican accent—and then it happened: she asked me what type of cancer I had. Suddenly all the research and information I had read, compiled, and digested in the past year came tumbling out of me as if I had been preparing for that moment for months, but it simply came straight from the heart. Never in a million years did I think I would have access to such a large stage and platform to talk about sarcoma, and that the information would pour from me so eloquently, but it happened. I held my own, I spoke my mind, and that was it. That was the sign I had been praying for from God and Papi; that was the sign I needed to understand why all this was happening. And I never again questioned if Artz Cure Sarcoma was my calling.

When I descended from the stage, one of Adele's staff handed me an iPhone to input my information, as while onstage Adele had promised me NY concert tickets. I was shaking so much that I didn't even know if I was typing in the right phone number. I had so much adrenaline coursing through my veins, I felt transported.

Everyone high-fived me as I walked back to my seat, and when I reached my girlfriend, we began to jump up and down like two teenagers. I was completely unaware that this incredible moment would soon become a viral video, opening the door to interviews on different platforms and allowing me to be a voice for sarcoma research. And that was when it dawned on me. I didn't need a celebrity advocate to help push my cause into the limelight; I could be the spokesperson for sarcoma. I had access to the media and could use this viral moment as the stepping-stone to an even bigger venture: at long last creating my Artz Cure Sarcoma Foundation.

A couple of weeks later, after all the hype had died down, I told Nick, "This is what I need to do." I no longer doubted that this was the right path. I was meant to do this. "I'm supposed to be an activist and the person to speak up and advocate for sarcoma patients."

All the struggles, all the lessons learned from dealing with so many doctors, the frustrations and complexities of the American health care system, had been like a master's degree program, preparing me to become a patient advocate for those who didn't have the means, information, or contacts to get the sarcoma treatment they needed. I needed to pursue this further. I hit the ground running, taking full advantage of the media storm that followed my viral video.

However, there was also another priority on my list: celebrating our third wedding anniversary. Since we hadn't been able to celebrate properly the previous year, given my diagnosis, I wanted to go all out for our third anniversary. We decided to visit Cuba, another country on our life list. The people, the culture, the food, the music, the art, the 1950s American cars, and of course the Cuban cigars. That trip truly blew us away. We were transported to a different era, a different way of life, where time had seemingly stood still.

As if the Adele experience followed by our incredible wedding anniversary journey weren't enough, when we got back home, I received the news that *People en Español* had selected me to be one of their 25 Mujeres Más Poderosas (25 Most Powerful Women). I had been chosen for my relentless activism to make an impact on the course of sarcoma treament, by creating global awareness of the disease, contributing to sarcoma research and my patient advocacy work.

But of course there was the little matter of my quarterly June checkup. So, again off to MD Anderson for the usual battery of tests. The results came back: NED. Another victory in my battle with sarcoma. I was still dealing with the ups and downs of Hashimoto's disease and IBS, but at least the cancer in my body was being held at bay.

As soon as I heard the news from *People en Español*, I went straight to work. I gathered a team of volunteers and told them it was time to bring Artz Cure Sarcoma to the next level and take advantage of all the upcoming media coverage. One of my friends turned our artzcuresarcoma.org website landing page into an actual website, and we found a donated venue for our second annual fund-raiser. I also continued to give interviews, was featured in different magazines, had photo shoots—nonstop action. I was physically exhausted but carried on because the work I was doing could save lives and help many. Those months buzzed with excitement and promise.

When the *People en Español*'s 25 Mujeres Más Poderosas issue launched, I walked the red carpet. As I did, I couldn't help but recall the little girl from Mayagüez, Puerto Rico, who, with the Spirit's guidance, confidence, and perseverance, reached for the stars by following her gut and intuition and made it!

At our second annual Artz Cure Sarcoma fund-raiser, I was struck by how the evening was a testament to the unwavering support from the art world and artists, the wine community, friends and family, and the Artz Cure Sarcoma volunteer team. Everyone had come together again in an even bigger and better way. More than two hundred guests attended in a jam-packed venue with tons of media coverage to help us make great strides in our efforts to build sarcoma awareness. Walking through the venue, greeting every guest, and admiring the artwork, my heart swelled with pride because I was spreading knowledge of sarcoma where little had existed, and I knew it was time. My very own LLC deserved to become a formal 501(c)(3).

I had experienced a roller-coaster eighteen months. Beginning with our trip to Istanbul, I had made the transition from cancer patient to patient advocate to fund-raiser. It had been one hell of a ride. But 2016 still had one more surprise in store for me—ticking off a very personal life list item I had dreamed of for a long time: attending a Chanel fashion show in Paris. Paris is my favorite city in the world, and seeing Karl Lagerfeld in person at one of his fashion shows was something I had always wanted to do since I was a young girl when he first joined Chanel. Gabrielle "Coco" Chanel's story has been a constant source of inspiration for me. Chanel defeated the odds: she was an orphan who turned her life around by following her passion and challenging the status quo. I have always been madly in love with Chanel's ready-to-wear items, fashion jewelry, shoes, handbags, and accessories. I have become one of their steadfast clients. They held a fashion show in Cuba, just days before our trip. I asked my Chanel fashion adviser at Bergdorf Goodman about the possibility of attending the show. He wasn't able to get me tickets for Cuba, but he said he could get me into the Spring/Summer 2016 show in Paris in October. My moment had finally arrived!

On October 4, 2016, Nick dropped me off at the Grand Palais in the City of Light and went to a café down the street to wait for me as I had only received one invite—no plus-one for this Chanel fashion show newbie. I walked in, dressed head to toe in Chanel, like everyone else, and bumped into major celebs. I was on cloud nine. As I took my seat, I noticed that *Vogue* editor Anna Wintour was a few seats down to my right, and I was in the presence of my fashion idol: Karl freaking Lagerfeld. I was a kid in a larger-than-life candy store—it was one what-the-hell moment if there ever was one for me. I couldn't help having a flashback to my teenage years when I would flip through my mom's fashion magazines, admiring the dresses that were seemingly unobtainable at the time and dreaming of Parisian runways—suddenly I was now part of that world and it made me realize how far the little girl from Sultana had come.

I felt as if my dad, God, and the universe had gotten together to show me that no matter how tough my journey got, no matter how many health issues I had to face, every second of life, of my life, is worth living—and that I was to continue living this way, no matter what.

14

Life List

Out of clutter, find simplicity.
From discord, find harmony.
In the middle of difficulty lies opportunity.

—ALBERT EINSTEIN

On our third date, Nick and I took it upon ourselves to create a life list, unaware of how that list of goals and dreams would become the driving force of our lives, especially during the lowest moments in our journey.

It provided light when we were traversing a forlorn and obscure tunnel of disease. It provided respite when we could no longer digest more medical information. It provided a safe haven when our world crashed down on us. It continues to provide hope when facing such an uncertain future.

While I continue to live my life enthusiastically, doing absolutely everything I am physically capable of accomplishing, it is no secret: my reality has changed. I now live with a cancer cloud that will hover over my head for the rest of my life and a voice inside wondering, *What if it comes back? What then?*

Nick and I talk about plans for our old age together even though both of us acknowledge that there's a chance I might not make it that far. I know these are difficult subjects to broach, but I refuse to live a life of denial, as some of my friends with cancer did. By the time they snapped out of their refusal to face the inevitable, it was too late.

The reality is that my organs have slowly been removed from my body. Oh, well, there goes the gallbladder; *adiós*, uterus, cervix, and fallopian tubes; *hasta la vista*, chunk of my rectum and anal muscle! It's as if I'm being emptied out. Same goes for the number of scars all over my body. Every scar has a story. How do I see it? I'm still standing. Does it stop me wearing a daring swimsuit? Hell no! I celebrate it.

Nick and I have never caught a break as a couple; except that we found each other and are still together. We've had to face obstacles and challenges from day one, but I didn't give up on Nick early on in our relationship because of Charles, and he hasn't given up on me as each illness has invaded. We remain solid and stable through the breathtaking highs and grueling lows. When I think of everything we've been through these past four years—hysterectomy, sarcoma, auto-immune diseases, surgeries, lupus, autoimmune retinopathy, Hashimoto's thyroiditis—I feel blessed because without this powerful gentleman by my side I would have given up. I shed tears of relief and happiness because of my absolute certainty that Nick is looking after me. That is a priceless feeling.

He picks me up when I'm down and reminds me of everything I have accomplished in my lifetime. He is my steadfast companion, who's wiped my tears, hugged me tight, loves me unconditionally, and witnessed my struggles. He has seen my failures and celebrated my successes. He has cheered me on and keeps me strong.

Nick is a man of honor—a man of his word. He has

proven over and over the vows he made on our wedding day. The words of the vows have taken on deeper meaning:

Zulema,
   I promise to be your lover and companion, and to laugh each day with you. I promise to help shoulder our challenges, for there is nothing we cannot face if we stand together. I promise to you perfect love and perfect trust. For one lifetime with you could never be enough. This is my sacred vow to you, my equal in all things.

Sarcoma was the ultimate wake-up call. A turning point. It was a pivotal moment that changed my perspective, shifted my priorities, and gave me a purpose in life. It was how God answered my prayer to be validated.

That turning point taught me it is okay to cut off toxic relationships and negative people, even people you have known almost your entire life. I have learned to forgive myself first, to stop carrying resentment. I have come to realize that the problem with those who disparage you has more to do with them.

I eliminated the surplus that doesn't add to my life. I've chosen to surround myself with positive people who are compassionate and mean well. I no longer fear what people will think of me. I am comfortable in my own skin. I am living my best life in my midforties. I live without regrets and without constantly looking at my past and dwelling on it. I surrendered, and then surrendered some more. I live more than ever in the present.

In my forty-six years, I've challenged the status quo. I've

gone against the grain of my family and what my culture dictates. I have been the outcast, the one who's rocked the boat more than once, the one who has aired her "dirty laundry," the one who hasn't conformed to social norms. I have stood up in the face of taboos and stigma by openly talking about anal cancer, my rectum, my vagina, my breasts, my uterus, and my cervix, while drinking champagne as if it comes out of the faucet.

I am an activist, a doer at heart, and have a fervent need to do all in my power to join forces with others to battle this rare type of cancer, whether it be through sharing my story or by raising funds and awareness for research. I want to deliver on what I promised: to change the course of this disease so that future generations won't have to struggle or die because they don't have chemo drugs. By sharing my story, I heal, and help others to heal too.

Artz Cure Sarcoma Foundation has given me a voice—the voice I was always meant to have. Often when people praise my work with sarcoma, my response is always the same: in giving to sarcoma research, I have received the best gift of all. The foundation has been my way of coping with my illness and has saved my sanity.

I have even been able to put my foundation to use during the greatest humanitarian crisis in my island's recent existence. When Hurricane María devastated Puerto Rico in September 2017, I pledged to allocate all Artz Cure Sarcoma Foundation funds raised from then until the end of the year to help bring medical aid relief to those in need on the island and to evacuate cancer patients requiring urgent treatment to the mainland—more meaningful than rolls of paper towels. I always acknowledge my roots, and helping the beautiful island I grew up on will always be part of who I am.

Colossal life changes bring learning. I have developed less patience and tolerance for small, avoidable inconveniences. I recognize who I can count on and trust and have vowed to forever cherish those kind, compassionate, and loving souls who surround me with their warmth and positivity. I have allowed myself to cry, laugh, face death, and, no matter what, hang on for dear life.

My medical journey is not over yet. It is a game of Twister filled with unknown moves that I am still in the process of discovering and understanding. My key to surviving on this uncertain path is to ride both the lows and the highs—between doctors' office visits and life list experiences, between being a patient and being a wife, between being the subject of my ailments and the spokesperson for them, all so that I can continue to feel that my life is still mine.

So, what's still pending on our life list?

- Climb Kilimanjaro in Africa. For our wedding we received Abercrombie & Kent gift certificates allowing us to tick off this life list item, but the hysterectomy, breast reconstruction, and subsequent sarcoma diagnosis put an end to that.
- Renew our ten-year wedding anniversary vows, a second wedding, at one of our favorite châteaus in France, with Jeff Leatham floral installations and Chef Yann Nury.
- Own an apartment in Paris to spend the summers in Europe and once and for all speak and write French fluently.

- Be a guest on the Ellen DeGeneres show to spread the word of sarcoma and dance with Ellen.
- Receive an honorary BS degree from Recinto Universitario de Mayagüez in Puerto Rico, from which I never graduated.
- Lunch with Oprah and her BFF, Gayle King. Oprah changed my life when I most needed it.
- First-row seats and backstage passes to a Tom Ford fashion show. Nick has accompanied me to the last two Chanel shows in Paris, but Tom Ford is one of his favorite designers.
- Be a guest speaker at the TED Talks conference in 2020.
- An Alexi Lubomirski photo shoot for Nick and me.
- Continue my piano lessons.
- Teach a short course at Yale University (my dream university) or give a commencement speech.
- Party during Mardi Gras in New Orleans.
- And ultimately, when we have accomplished everything we set out to do, buy a vineyard in Europe and retire making wine!

As part of my morning ritual, even before I brush my teeth, I thank God and Spirit for every new day of life that I am granted. I am living with fervent passion, thanking my angels and that voice inside for helping me to find Nick.

I have so much more: to do, to love, to live, to write, to dream, to eat, to drink, to buy, to travel, to laugh, to learn, to create, to teach, to heal, and to help!

There are no coincidences. The universe and Spirit have my back and yours too!

Afterword

SPIRITUAL AWAKENING

I am not afraid of death. I am not afraid of talking about death. I have faced death on more than one occasion. Furthermore, I openly acknowledge my life on earth might be more limited than others'. Death is the only certainty in our lives. Some may think that this acceptance, this ease stemmed from my sarcoma diagnosis, but it actually began much earlier. I realize now I began communicating with the dead, with Spirit, from a very young age.

I was born a psychic medium.

When I was five years old, I recall having a merry-go-round in the backyard on which I would spend hours on my own, spinning around while chatting with "people" I couldn't see or touch but could hear. I think my mom called them my imaginary friends.

When I was nine, I awoke one morning unable to shake from my mind the vivid dream I had had while sleeping. An ambulance had pulled up outside our house in the middle of the night and my grandfather Santiago had been carried in on a stretcher. My mom, my sister, and my aunt Ramona had then all said goodbye to him. I went to school that day with the dream constantly replaying in my head, in full color, like a scene from a movie. Almost twenty years later, I learned from Mami that my grandfather had not visited us that night. He suffered a massive stroke the following day while I was at school and died in the hospital. This was my first premonition—in full living color.

Growing up in Puerto Rico, I didn't know anyone who was a medium, nor would I have been allowed near someone who was. Even if I had dared to mention what I could see, feel, or hear, there was no way I would have been allowed to pursue my gift due to the strong Catholic influence and belief system in my family. I found out much later that there were other reasons, too, which I do not have time to go into here . . .

I have always felt that Spirit has guided me throughout my life. It led me to my husband, it has helped me navigate my medical challenges, and provided me with the support I needed when I hit rock bottom. But I always kept my gift hidden. If I had told anyone when I was growing up that I saw the dead or would constantly get messages from the dead, they would think I was crazy.

There was only one person I did tell—my husband. A few months after moving into our new apartment, I began to see apparitions of a man. The apparitions became steadily more frequent, more detailed, and accompanied by sounds. I would hear footsteps coming up the stairs and thinking it was Nick returning from work, call out to him, only to find no one there. One evening, I finally confided in him. I admit I was afraid of his reaction, but I shouldn't have been—he was super understanding, and—better yet—believed me. It was a relief to unburden myself of a secret I had kept for forty years. It turned out the apparitions I was experiencing were of the previous owner of the apartment, who had died of a heart attack on our living room floor and not in the Equinox gym as we had been told by the real estate agent. But don't worry, he has moved on now.

~

I finally got affirmation of my gift in January 2018, three days after my forty-fifth birthday. I met renowned psychic medium MaryAnn DiMarco for a one-on-one reading on camera that was being recorded for a television pilot. While the purpose of my being there was to connect with my relatives and a dear friend who had recently passed, and to get insight into my future as an author, deep down I wanted to know whether MaryAnn could affirm my medium abilities. Before the reading even began, as I was having a microphone put on me—and before I was introduced to MaryAnn—she had an immediate reaction.

"You are a medium, you are a psychic. Oh, I love reading psychic mediums. Are you finally going to accept that you are a psychic medium and not resist it?" she repeated over and over again.

MaryAnn brought me face-to-face with my gift. I couldn't deny it anymore. That day I felt as if I had been reborn. I felt a sense of peace unlike any I had experienced before, but I still needed to keep my psychic medium ability a secret until I figured things out.

In February 2018, at MaryAnn's suggestion, I visited Pat Longo, a healer, spiritual teacher, and mentor to Theresa Caputo, MaryAnn DiMarco, and many other bona fide mediums. After our initial meeting, I began to attend her mediumship practice sessions on Long Island. During the first of these meetings, I texted Nick in the middle of the session to say, "I now fully understand who I am. I've never felt more understood or been surrounded by people to whom I don't have to explain myself; they are like me." Pat has taught me how to use my gift and helped me to channel Spirit with greater precision and clarity. She remains instrumental in my psychic medium voyage.

The last twelve months have been yet another turning point in my life and a new journey on which I have embarked . . . there is so much more to do and so much more to share about my life as the Latina Medium.

Acknowledgments

I n July 2015 I asked a friend to introduce me to her agent, as I was now serious about publishing my book. A few weeks later the friend called me to say I had to self-publish because I wasn't a famous person; a large global publishing company wouldn't take a gamble on an unknown person like me. Oh, and no literary agent would sign me up because I didn't have a large social media following. Our friendship didn't last but it wasn't because of this. I want to thank and publicly acknowledge this former friend for firing up my determination to prove her wrong!

Firstly, my heart is filled with gratitude to Judith Curr and Johanna Castillo, the visionaries who approved my book proposal in April 2017. Although both Judith and Johanna left Atria Books in 2018, I am forever grateful to them for taking the risk of signing me, a new author without a literary agent. I had never published a book before but had big dreams. I know you both wholeheartedly believed in my story.

To the new team at Atria Books: Libby, the publisher, and Michelle, my senior editor: while the takeoff was rocky, we landed!

To my husband, Nick: your chicky-loopy girl's story had

to be heard. You never allowed me to settle for anything but the best. You put in an incredible number of hours into getting the manuscript to the right place. You were emotionally invested. As the book was nearing completion, you came down the stairs with tears in your eyes, saying chapter 2 made you cry. I knew if *you* cried, everyone else would too! You have inspired me to be the best version of me. I love you deeply, Mr. Bond.

To my nephew, Jam Jam, and niece, Marie: all I do is for you! Undoubtedly you are my kids even though I didn't give birth to you. All I want is to make you proud, to show you all the wonderful things life has to offer, to spoil you rotten, and to be your mentor, protector, and confidante. And one day, when you are both old enough, you'll get to hear Titi's life story directly from me.

To Mami: for all your love, being both mom and dad, looking after me during all of my surgeries, your awesome cooking, and being the best *abu* in the world. Your tenacity in overcoming adversity and your courage to always do the right thing has been an inspiration and guiding light in my life.

To Tío William: your love, sacrifices, and dedication to your family set the highest of bars. You are a rock star uncle and have made a tremendous impact on my life—and I cannot forget Mr. Jones, my favorite Welsh uncle.

To Ben: You saved me! There are no coincidences. The universe simply brought us together. Collaborating with you made the difference. Your can-do attitude under tight deadlines was a fresh breath of air at the most crucial moment.

To Stephen Palacios, my dear friend: You have been part of this book from even before I submitted a proposal. I vividly remember the cold December morning when you came over to our house to bounce ideas off each other, to craft an outline for the proposal, and as usual get into deep conversations about human behavior, cultural differences, and so much more.

To John Leonida and Stephen Palacios both: You were the only two people to read the manuscript. I valued every comment and revision you both suggested.

And to John, the most dapper British gentleman: I loved your sincerity the first time you read the book. You are brilliant, my friend! Absolutely brilliant! Thank you for carving out time from your hectic schedule and shipping the printed "magnum opus" with comments all the way from London!

To Luz María Doria, aka "La Mujer de Mis Sueños," executive producer of ¡*Despierta América!* on Univision: when I had temporarily shelved the book idea for a bit, you came into my life to reignite the fire in me to pursue it and make it a reality. That was your purpose. You were right, back in September 2016, when you told me I had to tell my story. Although the distance separates us, thank you for supporting my dreams. No dream is ever impossible!

To my dearest friend for nearly twenty years, Armando Correa, editor in chief of *People en Español*: little did I know the party at our home in October 2016 would be the catalyst that would make this book a reality. Thank you for the countless hours of advice, for letting me rant, for the lunches, phone calls, and text messages, and at times for being my shoulder to cry on. You kept me on the straight and narrow but were also sensitive and honest. I love you dearly, *mi querido* Mandy!

To Elisa Hernández, Beba: my childhood friend from Puerto Rico, who's stuck with me through thick and thin, and vice versa: thank you, *amiga*, for being compassionate, for understanding me, and for not judging or abandoning me when I was at my worst; instead you filled me with love and comprehension. *¡Te adoro, Beba!*

To Lea: my college BFF, who's my biggest cheerleader in anything I do. Thank *you*, dearest Lea! I mean, I could tell you I am climbing Kilimanjaro tomorrow without training, and you would tell me it is possible, that I will kill it, and that you'll come with me! Talk about someone having my back unconditionally and believing in me. I can't wait for our next chapter together—someday sipping bottomless bottles of champagne in my Parisian apartment!

To Fidel (sorry, I can't use his real name): for instilling the passion for literature and art in me as a young girl. Publishing this book is perhaps the only thing I've done ahead of you in life. I hope that you fulfill your dream of publishing your book. It's overdue!

To Dr. Janice Cormier: there are not enough days in the physical world to thank you for taking care of me and my health no matter what time of day and for coming to my rescue whenever I was unwell. You have been the doctor whose advice I could always trust. I feel safe with you as my oncologist. I feel loved. I feel cared for. And this is priceless. I am proud to call you my friend. Thank you for doing God's work by treating cancer patients with so much love and compassion.

To Dr. Keila Torres: I don't know how you do it. How you can operate on sarcoma patients, run the investigative soft-tissue sarcoma laboratory at MD Anderson Cancer Center, manage your foundation, care for your family, your husband, and your dogs, and be a photographer as well. You are a true wonder woman with a definite purpose in this life. Thank you for your friendship and educating me about sarcoma. Our work is just beginning. Fasten your seat belt!

Acknowledgments

To Dr. Craig Messick, my colorectal oncologist, and Dr. Mehnaz Shafi, my gastrointestinal oncologist, at MD Anderson Cancer Center: you both have a special place in my heart. Words can't express my gratitude. You are always there for me!

To Geraldine: you gave me wings when I needed to fly. Without you, getting to MD Anderson Cancer Center wouldn't have been possible. I am forever grateful. I promised you then that I'd pay it forward; I have, and I will continue to do so until it's my time to leave the physical world.

To Lisa: my dearest friend who crossed over. You have been by far the most significant loss of my adult life. Although we weren't of the same blood, you were my sister. We shared a common bond for the fine things in life, helping others, looking after our loved ones, and the "ups and downs" of powerful Latinas. I miss our time hanging out upstate, being neighbors, shopping together, and plotting our future. I realized that there would have never been enough time to prepare any of us for your departure. I thought I was the one dying; not you! Keep sending me signals from the other side. I love hearing from you.

To Cat Porter: my Chanel fairy, who has sprinkled and ignited my world with colossal Chanel ecstasy. You've proved that fairies do exist! Thank you for your friendship and our Parisian adventures.

To all the sarcoma volunteers, artists, donors, friends, and the media in the U.S. and Puerto Rico, who have helped me from day one: our work is not over.

To all our wine world friends, sommeliers, and producers: for all the special bottles opened and for the moments shared enjoying history in a liquid format.

To my awesome dear friends in Champagne, Alexandre Chartogne, Rodolphe Peters, Raphaël Bérêche, Olivier Krug,

Charles Phillipponnat, Fred Panaotis: Merci for letting me into your lives, for your friendship, and allowing me to leave a piece of my heart in the Champagne region.

To all the people I have met along the way—lovers, boyfriends, friends, former friends, colleagues, acquaintances, and doctors: you all had a purpose in my life and you all taught me something valuable. Thank you.

To Pat Longo and MaryAnn DiMarco, my spiritual teachers: I hope I make you proud in my mediumship voyage! You have both taught me how to serve others with honesty and love.

To all my loved ones who have crossed over to the other side and are lighting my life and steering me in the right direction.

To God, my angels, Spirit guides, and Spirit: thank you for showing me the path, day in and day out, even when the tough got tougher, because I believe there is a healing purpose for this book and that there was divine intervention every step of the way.